A Practical English Grammar
Structure Drills 2

A Practical English Grammar
Structure
Drills 2

A. J. Thomson
A. V. Martinet

Oxford University Press

033137

Oxford University Press
Walton Street, Oxford OX2 6DP

Oxford   New York   Toronto
Delhi   Bombay   Calcutta   Madras   Karachi
Petaling Jaya   Singapore   Hong Kong   Tokyo
Nairobi   Dar es Salaam   Cape Town
Melbourne   Auckland

and associated companies in
Beirut   Berlin   Ibadan   Nicosia

Oxford is a trade mark of Oxford University Press.

ISBN 0 19 431346 8
© Oxford University Press 1979, 1986

First published 1979
Reprinted three times
Fifth impression, reset with corrections, 1986
Seventh impression 1988

Typeset in Great Britain by
Promenade Graphics Limited, Cheltenham
Printed in Hong Kong

Contents

		page
Introduction		ix

like, hate, want, wish, prefer etc., mainly with gerund or infinitive

1	*like/liked*+gerund	1
2	*like/liked*+gerund, *wouldn't like/wouldn't care/would hate*+ infinitive	2
3	*like/dislike/hate/don't mind/don't care for/enjoy*+gerund	3
4	*prefer . . . to/like . . . better than*+gerund	4
5	*what about?*+gerund, *would rather*+infinitive without *to*, *would prefer*+infinitive	5
6	*would prefer*+object+infinitive, *would rather*+subject+past tense	6
7	*would like/want*+object+infinitive	7
8	*would like*+ perfect infinitive, *wanted*+present infinitive	8
9	*doesn't/didn't want*+object+infinitive	9
10	*wish*+infinitive	10
11	*wish*+subject+*would*, or *wish*+subject+past tense	11
12	*wish*+subject+past perfect tense	12

Verbs+gerunds

13	*admit/deny/be suspected of/be accused of/be charged with*	13
14	*avoid*	14
15	*enjoy*	15
16	*fancy/imagine*	16
17	*have*+object+*-ing* (present participle)	17
18	*couldn't help*	18
19	*keep*	19
20	*mean*	20
21	*would you mind*	21
22	*mind/object to*+*him/his*, *won't have*+*him*+*-ing* (present participle)	22
23	*prevent*+object+*(from)*	23
24	*remember*+gerund, *see/hear*+object+*-ing*	24
25	*remember*+*him/his* etc.	25
26	*stop*	26

27 *stop*+object+gerund   27
28 *suggest*   28
29 *suggest*   29
30 *suggest*+*them/their*   30
31 *try*   31
32 *want/need*   32

Gerunds after prepositions and certain expressions

33 *be afraid of/risk*   33
34 *be interested in*   34
35 *be/get used to*   35
36 *feel like*   36
37 *for* (*punish someone for/apologize for/get into trouble for*)   37
38 *have difficulty* (*in*)   38
39 *have difficulty in*+gerund, *find it easy*+infinitive   39
40 *it's no use/good, it's no use/good me/my*   40
41 *insist on, insist on me/my*   41
42 *in spite of*   42
43 *look forward to*   43
44 *make a point of*   44
45 *there's no point in, what's the point of*   45
46 *succeed in*+gerund, *manage*+infinitive   46

Infinitive without *to*, or present participle (*-ing*)

47 *hear*+object+*-ing*   47
48 *hear*+object+*-ing*   48
49 *hear*+object+*-ing*, or *hear*+object+infinitive without *to*   49
50 *see*+object+*-ing*   50
51 *see*+object+*-ing*, or *see*+object+infinitive without *to*   51
52 *see/hear*+object+*-ing*, or *see/hear*+object+infinitive without *to*   52
53 *see/hear*+object+*-ing*   53
54 *spend*+time+*-ing*   54

Infinitive without *to*

55 *had better*+infinitive without *to, it's time*+subject+past tense   55
56 *let*+object+infinitive without *to*   56
57 *let*+object+infinitive without *to*   57
58 *let*+object+infinitive without *to*   58
59 *make*+object+infinitive without *to*   59
60 *make*+object+infinitive without *to, be made*+infinitive with *to*   60

Verbs+(full) infinitive

61 *happen*+present and continuous infinitives   61
62 *mean*   62
63 *occur*+*to*+object+infinitive   63
64 *offer*   64
65 *remember/forget*   65
66 *seem*   66
67 *seem*+continuous infinitive   67
68 *seem/appear/is said/is supposed*+perfect infinitive   68
69 subject+*used*   69
70 subject+*used*   70

Infinitive constructions

71 *be afraid*   71
72 *be*+*horrified/glad/surprised/amazed/relieved* etc.   72
73 *it is/was*+adjective+*of*+object+infinitive   73
74 *what a/an*+adjective+noun+infinitive   74
75 *too*+adjective+infinitive, adjective+*enough*+infinitive   75
76 *too*+adjective+infinitive, adjective+*enough*+infinitive   76
77 *too*+adjective+infinitive, adjective+*enough*+infinitive   77

Purpose

78 Purpose expressed by the infinitive   78
79 *so as not*+infinitive   79
80 Purpose clauses and *prevent*+object+gerund   80
81 Purpose clauses: *so that*+subject+*would*   81
82 *in case*   82
83 *might*+perfect infinitive, *shouldn't*+perfect infinitive, *might/ shouldn't*+perfect infinitive   83

Passive

84 Simple present, simple past, present perfect and *should*   84
85 Present continuous and past continuous   85
86 Present perfect and past perfect   86
87 *may/might*+perfect infinitive   87
88 *must*+phrasal verbs   88
89 *should*+present and perfect infinitives   89
90 *used to*+infinitive   90
91 *will have/would have*+present infinitive   91

Reported/Indirect speech

92 Statements reported by *he says* or *he said*   92
93 *suggest*+gerund   93
94 Questions   94
95 Questions   95
96 *want*+object+infinitive   96
97 *advise/warn*+object+infinitive   97
98 Requests reported by *ask/want*+object+infinitive   98
99 Commands reported by *tell/warn/want*+object+infinitive, or
   say+subject+*be*+infinitive   99
100 Commands reported by *say*+subject+*be*+infinitive   100

Key   101

Introduction

These drills are based on our *Practical English Grammar*, and above most of them is given the number of the relevant paragraph of the *Grammar* (fourth edition, 1986), e.g. 'PEG 104'.

Like the exercises that also accompany the *Grammar*, the drills are graded ■, ◪ and □ in order of difficulty, ■ being the most difficult. The grading is printed to the left of the references.

Recordings of the drills are available from the publishers, but the book can also be used where a cassette-recorder or language laboratory is not available. All the prompt sentences are printed here, and the answers are printed in the key at the end of the book.

In most of the drills the student is required to answer or make a comment on a question or statement which he or she hears from the cassette or the teacher, e.g.

A: If I sell my car . . .
B: *Oh, are you thinking of selling your car?*

But in a few of the drills the sentence the student hears is merely a prompt which must be repeated in the answer, e.g.

A: I'm not late.
B: *I'm not late, am I?*

We have aimed at making these drills as much like ordinary conversation as possible, and in most cases the vocabulary has been kept deliberately simple. We hope that teachers and students will enjoy these drills and find them useful.

A.J.T., A.V.M.

1 like/liked + gerund

☐ PEG 295

(a) A (in tones of sympathy): You have to make beds, I suppose.
B (cheerfully): *Yes, but I like making beds!*

Twenty years later, Susan's children have left home, her husband has retired and they can afford some help in house and garden. Her friend reminds her of her former busy life.

(b) A: You had to make beds, I suppose.
B: *Yes, but I liked making beds!*

This exercise could also be done with (c) **don't/didn't mind** or (d) **enjoy/enjoyed**.

(a) *You have to . . . I suppose.*

1 do housework,
2 live economically,
3 shop around,
4 look after the children,
5 mend their clothes,
6 take them to school,
7 help them with their homework,
8 read to them,
9 answer their questions,
10 attend their school concerts,
11 watch them play football,
12 go swimming with them,
13 give children's parties,
14 meet your husband at the station, (*Use* **my**.)
15 listen to your husband's office stories, (*Use* **my**.)
16 entertain your husband's colleagues, (*Use* **my**.)
17 iron shirts,
18 knit pullovers,
19 weed the garden,
20 cut the grass,

(b) *You had to . . . I suppose.*

1 do housework,
2 live economically,
etc.

1

2 like/liked + gerund
wouldn't like/wouldn't care/would hate + infinitive

◪ PEG 295

Students' summer jobs.

This exercise should be done by students working in pairs. The prompt only is given and students must form both the question (A) and the answer (B). If it is not convenient to work in pairs, the teacher should take the part of the first student (A).

Prompt: drive lorries

(a) A: *You like driving lorries, don't you?*
 B: *Yes, but I wouldn't like/wouldn't care/would hate to drive lorries for a living.*

(b) A: *You liked driving lorries, didn't you?*
 B: *Yes, but I wouldn't like/wouldn't care/would hate to drive lorries for a living.*

enjoy/enjoyed could be used as well as **like/liked**.

Prompts:

1	sweep streets	11	pick fruit
2	mend roads	12	build houses
3	teach swimming	13	put up tents
4	conduct tours	14	paint railings
5	act as a guide	15	collect rubbish
6	guard factories	16	work in a factory
7	sell ice cream	17	deliver mail
8	serve in a shop	18	repair radios
9	dig drains	19	make cakes
10	wash windows	20	polish cars

3 like/dislike/hate/don't mind/don't care for/enjoy + gerund

☑ PEG 295

The life of an au pair.

A: I have to cook and wash up.

(a) B: *So have I. I like cooking but (I) hate washing up.*
(b) B: *So have I. I enjoy cooking but (I) don't care for washing up.*
(c) B: *So have I. I don't mind cooking but (I) dislike washing up.*

This drill can also be done in the past tense:

A: I had to cook and wash up.
B: *So had I. I liked cooking but (I) hated washing up.*

I have to . . .

1 hoover carpets and dust furniture.
2 make beds and clean rooms.
3 answer the door and answer the phone.
4 do the flowers and polish the silver.
5 buy fruit at the market and carry it home.
6 take the children to school and hurry home afterwards.
7 collect the children from school and supervise their homework.
8 talk to the children and teach them French.
9 go to the beach with the children and play in the sand.
10 put the children to bed and tidy up after them.
11 look after the baby and share a room with him.
12 give the baby his bath and wash his clothes.
13 drive the car and exercise the pony.
14 walk the dogs and brush them.
15 attend classes and do homework.

4 prefer . . . to/like . . . better than + gerund

☑ PEG 297

A: My brother plays tennis but hardly ever watches it.

(a) B: *My brother prefers playing (tennis) to watching (it) too.* (slight stress on **my**)

(b) B: *My brother likes playing (tennis) better than watching (it) too.* (slight stress on **my**)

My brother . . .

1 sings in a choir but hardly ever sings solo.
2 talks; he hardly ever listens.
3 drinks (at parties) but hardly ever dances.
4 spends money but hardly ever saves it.
5 phones; he hardly ever writes.
6 listens to the radio; he hardly ever watches TV.
7 mows the lawn but hardly ever weeds the garden.
8 paints pictures; he hardly ever takes photographs.
9 takes taxis; he hardly ever waits for a bus. (*Use* **buses.**)
10 drives; he hardly ever lets me drive.
11 cycles; he hardly ever walks.
12 eats out; he hardly ever cooks for himself.
13 stays at home (for his holidays); he hardly ever goes abroad.
14 rushes about (during his holidays); he hardly ever relaxes.
15 takes people to restaurants; he hardly ever invites them to his house.

5 what about? + gerund, would rather + infinitive without to would prefer + infinitive

◪ PEG 289B, 297

In this drill the prompt only is given and students must form both the question (A) and the answer (B). Students could work in pairs, one being A and the other B.

Prompt: walk on . . . wait for a bus

    A: *What about walking on? Or would you rather wait for a bus?*

(a) B: *I'd rather walk on (than wait for a bus).* (Words in brackets may be omitted.)

(b) B: *I'd prefer to walk on.*

This drill could also be done with **I'm against/for** or **I'm in favour of** + gerunds:

(c) B: *I'm against waiting for a bus.*

(d) B: *I'm for waiting for a bus.*

(e) B: *I'm in favour of waiting for a bus.*

(The speaker in (d) and (e) does not agree with the speaker in (a), (b) and (c).)

Prompts:

1 write . . . phone
2 cook it . . . eat it raw
3 camp . . . stay in a hotel
4 deliver it by hand . . . post it
5 drive . . . fly
6 mend the old one . . . buy a new one
7 go as we are . . . change into evening dress
8 get a job . . . ask our parents to send us money
9 finish it tonight . . . leave it till tomorrow
10 try to fix it ourselves . . . send for an electrician
11 wash the sheets at home . . . take them to the launderette
12 do our own typing . . . employ a secretary
13 tune the piano ourselves . . . get a piano tuner
14 borrow a TV set . . . hire one
15 buy a cat . . . put down rat poison
16 ring the dentist today . . . put it off till tomorrow
17 start now . . . wait for Bill
18 hitch-hike . . . cycle
19 stay at home next weekend . . . go away
20 keep some . . . eat it all now

6 would prefer + object + infinitive
would rather + subject + past tense

◪ PEG 297

(i)

A: Shall I phone Tom tomorrow?
(a) B: *I'd prefer you to phone him today.*
or
(b) B: *I'd rather you phoned him today.*

(ii)

A: Shall I show Tom the photographs tomorrow?
(a) B: *I'd prefer you to show them to him today.* (Note word order.)
or
(b) B: *I'd rather you showed them to him today.* (Note word order.)

Shall I . . . tomorrow?

 1 phone Bill
 2 bring my friends
 3 speak to James
 4 sweep the stairs
 5 begin
 6 pay the milk bill
 7 come
 8 leave
 9 go to the library (*Omit* **to the library.**)
10 read the instructions
11 lend Peter the map (*See* (ii) *above.*)
12 take the books back
13 give Ann your message (*See* (ii) *above.*)
14 burn the rubbish
15 send Peter the cheque (*See* (ii) *above.*)
16 get the new programme
17 write to the Smiths
18 see to the electric iron
19 buy your season ticket
20 make the arrangements

6

7 would like/want + object + infinitive

☑ PEG 296

(a) A: Would you like to make a speech?
B: *No, I'd like you to make a speech.* (stress on **you**)

(b) A: Do you want to make a speech?
B: *No, I want you to make a speech.* (stress on **you**)

(a) *Would you like to . . .*   (b) *Do you want to . . .*

1 lead the deputation?
2 pick the team?
3 receive the mayor?
4 speak first?
5 introduce the speakers?
6 sign the cheque?
7 witness Tom's signature?
8 engage the extra staff?
9 appoint a press officer?
10 attend the conference?
11 give a talk?
12 meet the president?
13 make the arrangements?
14 answer any queries?
15 choose the colours?
16 supervise the painters?
17 make the arrangements?
18 fix a date?
19 organize the reception?
20 open the champagne?

8 would like + perfect infinitive, wanted + present infinitive

☑ PEG 296

A: Did you see the castle?

(a) B: *No, I would like to have seen it* but there wasn't time.*

(b) B: *No, I wanted to see it but there wasn't time.*

*Note: **would have liked to see it** and **would have liked to have seen it** are also possible forms.

Did you . . .

1 ring Peter?
2 talk to the students?
3 attend the conference?
4 try the beer?
5 watch the match?
6 visit the museum?
7 see the zoo?
8 walk round the town?
9 meet your friends?
10 look at the old bridge?
11 climb to the top of the monument?
12 have coffee? (Answer with **some.**)
13 paint any pictures? (**some**)
14 make a sketch? (Answer with **one.**)
15 take any photographs? (**some**)
16 hire a boat? (**one**)
17 stroll round the market?
18 send any postcards? (**some**)
19 buy any souvenirs? (**some**)
20 listen to the town band?

9 doesn't/didn't want + object + infinitive

☑ PEG 296C

Ann is a young married woman with a lot of time on her hands. Two of her friends think that she would be happier if she had an occupation or hobby. Unfortunately her husband doesn't seem to share their views.

(a) A: Have you suggested going to evening classes?
B: *Yes, but apparently her husband doesn't want her to go to evening classes.* (stress on **want**)
or
A: Did you suggest going to evening classes?
B: *Yes, but apparently her husband doesn't want her to go to evening classes.* (It is still a present problem.)

(b) A: Did you suggest going to evening classes?
B: *Yes, but apparently her husband didn't want her to go to evening classes.* (It is now a *past* problem.)

Have you suggested . . .

1 painting?
2 riding?
3 working in the garden?
4 taking a driving test?
5 making friends with her neighbours?
6 inviting her mother to stay?
7 getting a part-time job?
8 hiring a typewriter?
9 joining a drama club?
10 acting in a play?
11 singing in the choir?
12 buying a dog?
13 helping at the old people's club?
14 studying Russian?
15 learning judo?
16 attending keep-fit classes?
17 going to art lectures?
18 taking a course in vegetarian cooking?
19 redecorating the house?
20 training as a tourist guide?

10 wish + infinitive

☐ PEG 299

Alan is a newcomer; Bill is an old hand.

A: How does one set about complaining about something?
B: *Oh, just go to the office and say you wish to complain about something.*

(**want** or **would like** could also be used, of course. **wish** is the most formal of the three.)

How does one set about . . .

1 enrolling for a course?
2 making a complaint?
3 reporting an accident?
4 seeing the welfare officer?
5 taking a test?
6 applying for study leave?
7 entering for an exam?
8 joining the union?
9 starting a club?
10 arranging a football match?
11 organizing a trip?
12 hiring a coach?
13 having a poster printed?
14 insuring one's life? (*Use* **your.**)
15 paying one's fees? (*Use* **your.**)
16 moving to another branch?
17 voting in the election?
18 claiming compensation?
19 changing one's department (*Use* **your.**)
20 resigning?

11 wish + subject + would, or wish + subject + past tense

◪ PEG 300

Peter is a student who lives in a flat quite near his parents' house. His parents quite often visit his flat, but are not very impressed by the way he keeps it.

A: Peter is very bad about making his bed.

(a) B: *Yes, I wish he'd make it more regularly.* (= I wish he were willing to make it more regularly.)

(b) B: *Yes, I wish he made it more regularly.* (= I'm sorry he doesn't make it more regularly.)

Peter is very bad about . . .

1 paying the milkman.
2 cleaning his bath.
3 tidying up.
4 defrosting his fridge.
5 changing his sheets.
6 sweeping his room.
7 washing his shirts.
8 cutting his hair.
9 shaving.
10 doing the washing up.
11 putting his milk bottles out.
12 cooking for himself.
13 opening his windows.
14 emptying his ashtrays.
15 attending classes.
16 writing essays.
17 answering letters.
18 having his clothes cleaned.
19 taking his library books back.
20 watering his geraniums.

12 **wish** + subject + past perfect tense

■ PEG 300

After the accident.

A: Why didn't you help him?
B: *I don't know. I wish I had helped him.*

A: Why did you refuse to help him?
B: *I don't know. I wish I hadn't refused to help him.*

Why . . .

1 did you go into the pub?
2 did you allow him to drink so much?
3 didn't you make him eat something?
4 did you agree to drive home with him?
5 didn't you tell him he was too drunk to drive?
6 didn't you leave the car in the car park?
7 didn't you lock the car?
8 didn't you hide the key?
9 did you say you were in a hurry?
10 didn't you wait till he was sober?
11 didn't you ring me?
12 didn't you offer to drive yourself?
13 didn't you insist on driving?
14 did you get in with him?
15 didn't you refuse to go with him?
16 didn't you wait for a bus?
17 didn't you warn him about the ice?
18 did you let him go so fast?
19 didn't you remind him about the level crossing?
20 didn't you fasten your seat belt?

13 admit/deny/be suspected of/be accused of/be charged with + gerund

□ PEG 261

A: Did he say he had stolen the documents?
(a) B: *Yes, he admitted stealing them.*
(b) B: *No, he denied stealing them.*
(c) B: *No, but he is suspected of stealing them.*
(d) B: *No, but he has been accused of/charged with stealing them.*

Did he say he had . . .

1 forged the signature?
2 planned the hold-up?
3 taken part in the robbery?
4 hijacked the plane?
5 kidnapped the heiress?
6 fired at the policeman?
7 attacked the cashier?
8 shot the chauffeur?
9 threatened the Prime Minister?
10 sent the letter bombs?
11 received the stolen goods?
12 sold the secret information?
13 given false evidence? (*Keep* **false evidence.**)
14 intimidated the witnesses?
15 bribed the officials?
16 started the fires?
17 derailed the train?
18 led the raid?
19 drugged the guards?
20 helped the prisoners to escape? (*Keep* **to escape.**)

14 avoid + gerund

☐ PEG 261

An old man is talking to his doctor.

A: I travelled overnight and felt awful afterwards.
B: *Then try to avoid travelling overnight.*

I . . . and felt awful afterwards.

1 got very angry
2 overate
3 drank too much
4 went to bed too late
5 rushed about
6 stood for a long time
7 made a long speech (*Use* **speeches.**)
8 read in a bad light
9 carried a heavy suitcase (*Use* **suitcases.**)
10 played cards all night
11 took sleeping pills
12 travelled by jet
13 worked all weekend
14 quarrelled with my neighbours
15 slept in a haunted room (*Use* **rooms.**)

15 enjoy + gerund

☐ PEG 261

A: I had a lovely time yesterday; I wrote letters all day.
B: *Do you actually enjoy writing letters?* (stress on **enjoy**)

I had a lovely time yesterday. I . . . all day.

1 peeled potatoes
2 washed windows
3 mended socks
4 cleaned shoes
5 sewed on buttons
6 ironed shirts
7 patched sheets
8 polished the silver (*Omit* **the.**)
9 played with the children (*Omit* **the.**)
10 practised the piano
11 worked in the garden
12 cooked
13 baked
14 watched cricket
15 looked after children
16 baby-sat
17 dyed curtains
18 rearranged the furniture (*Omit* **the.**)
19 chopped wood
20 house-hunted

16 fancy/imagine + gerund

◪ PEG 261

A: She doesn't go to bed at all!
B: *Fancy not going to bed at all!*
or
B: *Imagine not going to bed at all!*

A: She abandoned her baby!
B: *Fancy abandoning one's/your baby!*
or
B: *Imagine abandoning one's/your baby!*

1 My sister doesn't enjoy her days off.
2 Tom doesn't know his own age.
3 Bill refused a rise in salary.
4 She was an au pair girl for ten years.
5 She never has a night out.
6 She baby-sits every night.
7 They paid £50 for a single meal.
8 They watch television for thirty hours a week.
9 The mother doesn't know where her baby is.
10 She got married at fourteen.
11 She waited twenty years for him. (*Omit* **for him.**)
12 He works a 70-hour week.
13 He lost all his savings.
14 They keep a snake as a pet.
15 He spends his holidays looking for fossils.
16 He was dismissed for working too hard.
17 He won £50,000.
18 He spent a month underground.
19 They queued all night.
20 He didn't want to leave prison.

17 **have** + object + **-ing** (present participle)

◪ PEG 121A

The confident instructor.

A: How long will it take me to learn to read music?
B: *I'll have you reading music by the end of the month.*

How long will it take me to learn to . . .

1 skate?
2 ski?
3 ride?
4 dance?
5 swim?
6 dive?
7 drive?
8 type?
9 write shorthand?
10 cook?
11 paint?
12 speak in public?
13 play the flute?
14 talk English?
15 walk again?
16 surf-ride?
17 canoe?
18 sail?
19 glide?
20 relax?

18 couldn't help + gerund

☐ PEG 261

A (accusingly): You got lost!
B: *I couldn't help getting lost.*

1–10 John wanted Bill to remain absolutely still. Bill, however, couldn't manage this.

You . . .

1 coughed!
2 sneezed!
3 laughed!
4 shivered!
5 smiled!
6 blinked!
7 moved!
8 sighed!
9 yawned!
10 fell asleep!

11–20 Ann is just generally disapproving of Bill's actions. (Keep nouns unchanged.)

You . . .

11 came in late.
12 made a noise.
13 disturbed us all.
14 woke the people in the next flat.
15 caught a cold.
16 got into debt.
17 heard their conversation.
18 saw what was in the letter.
19 trod on my toe.
20 kissed her.

19 keep + gerund

☐ PEG 261

The new secretary isn't a great success. A colleague tries to defend her but the boss is clearly very dissatisfied.

A: It isn't very terrible to break a cup now and then.
B: *But she keeps breaking cups.* (stress on **keeps**)

It isn't very terrible to . . . now and then.

1 come late
2 go home early
3 take time off
4 make mistakes
5 mix up appointments
6 lose documents
7 argue
8 answer back
9 interrupt
10 leave the safe open
11 forget to switch the lights off
12 yawn
13 look out of the window
14 wave to people in the street
15 ring up one's friends (*Use* **her.**)
16 ask for days off
17 retire to the cloakroom
18 have headaches
19 switch on one's radio (*Use* **her.**)
20 spell your name wrong (*Use* **my.**)

20 mean + gerund

☑ PEG 261

Alan is planning an uncomfortable expedition. Bill isn't enthusiastic.

(a) A: We'll have to walk twenty miles a day.
    B: *Well, I won't come if it means walking twenty miles a day.*

Other possible answers are: *But I object to/don't like/dislike/hate/detest walking twenty miles a day.*

This drill could also be used for **be/get used to** + gerund exercises, as in Drill 35.

(b) A: We'll have to walk twenty miles a day.
    B: *But I'm not used to walking twenty miles a day.*

Here Bill speaks first:

(c) A: You want me to walk twenty miles a day?
    B: *Yes. You'll soon get used to walking twenty miles a day.*

Bill has joined the expedition and isn't finding it too disagreeable. A friend sympathizes, but Bill doesn't want sympathy.

    A: You have to walk twenty miles a day? How awful!
(d) B: *Oh, I'm getting used to walking twenty miles a day.*
(e) B: *Oh, you soon get used to walking twenty miles a day.*
(f) B: *Oh, I've got used to walking twenty miles a day.*
(g) B: *Oh, I soon got used to walking twenty miles a day.*

Note that (c) – (g) require slight changes in the original sentences spoken by A.

We'll have to . . .

1 get up at five.	11 climb mountains.
2 set off at dawn.	12 camp in the snow.
3 tell no one where we're going.	13 cross frontiers secretly.
4 hitch-hike.	14 travel with forged documents.
5 row across the Channel.	15 use false names.
6 cycle for hundreds of miles.	16 make parachute landings.
7 carry heavy rucksacks.	17 sleep under bridges.
8 swim across lakes.	18 march in demonstrations.
9 wade through swamps.	19 stow away in a cargo ship.
10 canoe down rivers.	20 live on dried beans.

21 would you mind + gerund

☐ PEG 263

(a) A: Someone will have to get maps.
   B: *Yes. Would you mind getting them?* (slight stress on **you**)

(b) A: Someone will have to put the milk bottles out.
   B: *Yes. Would you mind putting them out?* (Notice word order.) (slight stress on **you**)

Someone will have to . . .

1 make sandwiches.
2 fill the thermoses.
3 keep an eye on the children.
4 buy maps.
5 work out our route. (*See* (b) *above.*)
6 pick up the traveller's cheques. (*See* (b) *above.*)
7 book the rooms.
8 look after the passports.
9 put on the roof rack. (*See* (b) *above.*)
10 arrange the insurance.
11 tell the neighbours we're going away.
12 stop the milk.
13 defrost the fridge.
14 pack for the children.
15 lock the cases.
16 bring the luggage down to the hall.
17 ask Mrs Jones to forward our letters.
18 amuse the children during the journey.
19 map-read.
20 tidy up.

22 mind/object to + him/his + gerund
won't have + him + -ing (present participle)

☑ PEG 121B, 262, 263

Tom, who has a very relaxed attitude to work, has just joined the staff. A senior employee, shocked by his behaviour, points out his 'crimes' to the manager. But the manager, who is about to retire, doesn't mind much.

A (in shocked tones): He kisses your secretary!

(a) B: *Oh, I don't mind him* kissing my secretary!*

But when this manager resigns and a new man is appointed, things are going to be different.

A: He kisses your secretary!

(b) B: *I object to him* kissing my secretary!*
(c) B: *I won't have him kissing my secretary!*

***his** is technically the more correct form, but **him** is more usual in spoken English.

He . . .

1 borrows from the petty cash!
2 spends two hours having lunch!
3 writes his own letters during office hours!
4 gets your secretary to type his private letters!
5 arrives late!
6 goes home early!
7 takes a day off when he feels like it!
8 wears jeans!
9 chews gum!
10 puts his feet on the desk!
11 sleeps at his desk!
12 phones his friends from the office!
13 argues with clients!
14 goes barefoot in hot weather!
15 parks his motor cycle in the hall!
16 drops ash on the carpet!
17 leaves burning cigarettes about!
18 smokes your cigars!
19 uses the company car at weekends!
20 chases your secretary round the office! (*Use* **my**.)

23 prevent + object + (from) + gerund

☑ PEG 261

Next to Tom's house is a nice open, grassy place, where people come for picnics. This annoys Tom, but his friend explains that he can't do anything to stop it.

1–10
A (angrily): They park here!
B (soothingly): *It's very difficult to prevent people parking here.* (slight stress on **prevent**)

11–20
A: Their children trample on my flowers!
B: *It's very difficult to prevent children trampling on flowers.* (*Omit* **their** and **my.**)

1–10 *They* . . .

1 have picnics here!
2 light fires!
3 leave litter!
4 bang their car doors!
5 make a horrible noise!
6 lie about almost naked!
7 use terrible language!
8 play their radios loudly!
9 fry sausages!
10 bring hordes of children!

11–20 *Their children* . . .

11 shout and scream!
12 carve their names on the trees! (*Omit* **the.**)
13 write things on my walls! (*Omit* **my.**)
14 kick their footballs over my walls! (*Omit* **my.**)
15 climb over my walls! (*Omit* **my.**)
16 pick my flowers! (*Omit* **my.**)
17 steal my fruit! (*Omit* **my.**)
18 swing on my gates! (*Omit* **my.**)
19 look through my windows! (*Omit* **my.**)
20 dash round on bicycles!

24 remember + gerund, see/hear + object +-ing

☐ PEG 268, 273

Peter annoyed his host, but doesn't remember much about the party.

(a) A: He says you spoilt his party.
   B: *I don't remember spoiling his party.* (slight stress on 'I')

Another guest witnessed Peter's terrible behaviour. Here Peter speaks first.

(b) A: I didn't arrive drunk!
   B: *Oh yes, you did. I saw you arriving drunk!*

   A: I didn't swear at him!
   B: *Oh yes, you did. I heard you swearing at him!*

Use **heard** or **saw**, whichever seems logical.

See also Drills 50–3.

(a) *He says you . . .*

1 arrived drunk.
2 brought two drunk friends.
3 refused to leave.
4 shouted at him.
5 swore at him.
6 called him names.
7 broke a decanter.
8 drank half a bottle of gin.
9 started a fight.
10 danced on the table.
11 upset a bookcase.
12 sang terrible songs.
13 made an awful lot of noise.
14 woke the people in the next flat.
15 insulted the Lord Mayor.
16 annoyed all the other guests.
17 burnt holes in his carpet.
18 spilt wine on his dinner jacket.
19 invited everyone to your country house (*Use* **my**.)
20 fell down the front steps.

(b) *I didn't . . .*

1 arrive drunk.
2 bring *etc., as in* (a)
3 refuse . . .
4 shout . . .
5 swear . . .
6 call . . .
7 break . . .
8 drink . . .
9 start . . .
10 dance . . .
11 upset . . .
12 sing . . .
13 make . . .
14 wake . . .
15 insult . . .
16 annoy . . .
17 burn . . .
18 spill . . .
19 invite . . .
20 fall . . .

25 remember + him/his etc. + gerund

☐ PEG 262, 268

Paul didn't enjoy his holiday. But Ann doesn't seem to remember the various disasters.

A: Breakfast was late.
B: *I don't remember it/its being late.*

Use pronoun object: it, **him, her, you, them,** or possessive adjective: **its, his, her, your, their.**

1 The receptionist was rude. (*Use* **her.**)
2 The people opposite sang all night.
3 They forgot to bring our early morning tea.
4 They refused to clean my car.
5 The lift broke down.
6 The kitchen staff went on strike.
7 I lost my camera. (*Use* **you/your.**)
8 The other guests got drunk every night.
9 The bed creaked.
10 The windows rattled.
11 Our bedroom was draughty.
12 They ran out of ice.
13 The radiators whistled.
14 The taxi drivers cheated us.
15 It rained nearly all the time.
16 The hall porter insulted me.
17 I suffered from food poisoning.
18 The hotel overcharged us.
19 They mixed up our reservations.
20 I was stung by a jellyfish.

26 stop + gerund

☑ PEG 270

A disagreeable flat-mate.

A: He drinks methylated spirits.
(a) B: *You should tell him to stop drinking methylated spirits.*
(b) B: *Why don't you tell him to stop drinking methylated spirits?*
(c) B: *Can't you get him to stop drinking methylated spirits?*
(d) B: *Can't you stop him drinking methylated spirits?*

He . . .

1 argues all the time.
2 chews tobacco.
3 sleepwalks.
4 talks to himself.
5 follows me about.
6 listens to my telephone conversations.
7 annoys the neighbours.
8 hangs his washing out of the window.
9 borrows my things.
10 uses bad language.
11 parks outside my garage.
12 steals my apples.
13 burns rubbish in the garden.
14 drops banana skins on the steps.
15 opens my letters.
16 is rude to my friends.
17 pulls the cat's tail.
18 looks through keyholes.
19 smokes marijuana.
20 plays the radio all night.

27 stop + object + gerund

◪ PEG 270

A: He spoke at street corners. His mother blamed me for it. (stress on **me**)

B: *But how could you stop him speaking at street corners?* (stress on **stop** or **you**)

He . . . His mother blamed me for it.

1 left home.
2 gave up shaving.
3 grew his hair.
4 threw away his suits.
5 went about barefoot.
6 wore ragged jeans.
7 tore up his passport.
8 resigned his job.
9 lived on National Assistance.
10 squatted in an empty house.
11 got married.
12 started a family.
13 played the guitar in the Underground.
14 led protest marches.
15 carried banners.
16 invited other squatters to join him.
17 barricaded the door.
18 changed the locks.
19 insulted the owners.
20 resisted arrest.

28 suggest + gerund

☐   PEG 289C,D

A: Why didn't you go to his flat?
B: *Well, Ann suggested going to his flat but I didn't think it was necessary.* (slight stress on 'I')

Why didn't you . . .

1 record his conversation?
2 ask him for proof of his identity?
3 look at his passport?
4 consult a solicitor?
5 discuss it with me? (*Use* **you.**)
6 wait a few weeks?
7 check his figures?
8 have the document translated?
9 show the letter to a handwriting expert?
10 read the small print?
11 find out where he had worked before?
12 make some enquiries about him?
13 ring his previous employers?
14 give him a post-dated cheque?
15 contact his embassy?
16 take his photograph?
17 get his fingerprints?
18 follow him home?
19 tap his phone?
20 bug his room?

29 suggest + gerund

☐   PEG 289C,D

A: Why didn't you hitch-hike home?
B: *Well, I suggested hitch-hiking home but Tom wouldn't hear of it.*

See also Drill 93.

Why didn't you . . .

1 leave at once?
2 look for a cheaper hotel?
3 demand a refund?
4 see the manager?
5 complain to the agency?
6 hire a caravan?
7 borrow a tent?
8 sleep on the beach?
9 pawn your watches? (*Use* **our.**)
10 try your luck at the casino? (*Use* **our.**)
11 get a job in a restaurant?
12 offer to work as guides?
13 sell your cameras? (*Use* **our.**)
14 report the matter to the police?
15 ask your consul for help? (*Use* **our.**)
16 ring me? (*Use* **our.**)
17 tell your parents? (*Use* **our.**)
18 consult a lawyer?
19 refuse to pay?
20 make a fuss?

30 suggest + them/their + gerund

☑ PEG 289D

Peter's friends have been harassing a business rival. Their victim complains to Peter, who disclaims responsibility.

    A: They dyed their hair. Apparently it was your idea.
(a) B: *I never suggested them/their dying their hair!* (slight stress on 'I')

This exercise could also be done with

(b) *I never suggested that they (should) dye their hair!*
(c) *I never suggested that they dyed their hair!*
    or
(d) *I never told/advised them to dye their hair!*

They . . . Apparently it was your idea.

1 wore masks.
2 carried guns.
3 pretended to be gunmen.
4 forged my signature. (*Use* **your.**)
5 sent me anonymous letters. (*Use* **you.**)
6 threatened me. (*Use* **you.**)
7 tried to blackmail me. (*Use* **you.**)
8 bribed my secretary. (*Use* **your.**)
9 tapped my phone. (*Use* **your.**)
10 bugged my office. (*Use* **your.**)
11 broke into my factory. (*Use* **your.**)
12 forced open my safe. (*Use* **your.**)
13 stole the week's takings.
14 burnt secret documents.
15 tore up my clients' letters.
16 erased tapes.
17 threw my electric typewriter out of the window. (*Use* **your.**)
18 wrecked the computer.
19 wrote slogans on the walls.
20 poured paint over my car. (*Use* **your.**)

31 try + gerund

☐ PEG 270

A: Do you think it would help if we pressed the red button?
B: *Yes, let's try pressing the red button.*

Do you think it would help if we . . .

1 oiled the hinges?
2 nailed the stair carpet down?
3 put the cake back in the oven?
4 cut the sandwiches the day before?
5 ate less fat?
6 took more exercise?
7 opened the windows?
8 turned down the central heating?
9 moved the piano to another room?
10 locked the doors at night?
11 painted the ceiling dark green?
12 paid the bills weekly?
13 filled the radiator with hot water?
14 blocked up all the rat holes?
15 cooked it in oil?
16 left the saucepan lid off?
17 soaked the beans a bit longer?
18 whipped the cream?
19 washed it in cold water?
20 stood on our heads for a few minutes?

32 want/need + gerund

☐ PEG 267E

A: You should tidy the garden.
B: *Yes, it wants/needs tidying.*

You should . . .

1 paint your windows.
2 polish the door knocker.
3 sweep the steps.
4 cut the grass.
5 weed the flower beds.
6 water the roses.
7 pick the peaches.
8 spray your lettuces.
9 clip the hedge.
10 rebuild your wall.
11 tie up the creeper.
12 mend the fence.
13 rake the path.
14 dig the potato patch.
15 prune the apple trees.
16 cut off the dead branches.
17 net the raspberries.
18 roll the lawn.
19 prop up the old pear tree.
20 clean out the birdbath.

33 be afraid of/risk + gerund

☐ PEG 261, 271A

Alan and Bill are discussing certain actions by Tom. Alan suggests a reason for them and Bill agrees.

A: I expect he didn't want to get wet.
(a) B: *Yes, I suppose he was afraid of getting wet.*
(b) B: *Yes, he probably didn't want to risk getting wet.*

Compare with Drill 71, *be afraid to.*

I expect he didn't want to . . .

1 miss the train.
2 overload the car.
3 get a parking ticket.
4 have his licence endorsed.
5 be sent to prison.
6 annoy the boss.
7 lose his job.
8 break his neck.
9 make things worse.
10 wake everyone up.
11 cause an accident.
12 press the wrong button.
13 touch a live wire.
14 electrocute himself.
15 cause a scandal.
16 upset his wife.
17 catch cold.
18 spoil his new suit.
19 shock the neighbours.
20 attract attention.

34 be interested in + gerund

☐ PEG 259

George wants Bill to co-operate with him and offers all sorts of inducements. But Bill is not ambitious.

A: You might make a lot of money!
B: *But I'm not interested in making a lot of money.*

You might . . .

1 become a celebrity!
2 be invited to marvellous parties!
3 meet important people!
4 get an honorary degree!
5 appear on television!
6 take part in radio programmes!
7 influence public opinion!
8 travel first class all over the world!
9 go on lecture tours!
10 see your name in lights!
11 employ a large staff!
12 live in luxury!
13 drive a Rolls Royce!
14 buy an island in the Pacific!
15 marry two or three times!

35 be/get used to + gerund

☑ PEG 163

A new employee is being told about his job.

(a) A: You'll have to sleep by the phone. All right?
    B: *Yes, I'm used to sleeping by the phone.*

A similar interview, but with a different employee. Here the employee speaks first.

(b) A (horrified): You expect me to sleep by the phone!
    B: *Yes, but you'll soon get used to sleeping by the phone.*

This man takes the job and doesn't find it as bad as he expected. A friend sympathizes unnecessarily:

(c) A: You have to sleep by the phone!
    B: *Oh, I'm getting used to sleeping by the phone.*
(d) B: *Oh, I've got used to sleeping by the phone.*
(e) B: *Oh, I soon got used to sleeping by the phone.*
(f) B: *Oh, you soon get used to sleeping by the phone.*

Other possible answers to (a) are *Yes, I don't mind sleeping/don't object to sleeping* etc., or: *But I'm not used to sleeping/object to sleeping* etc.

You'll have to . . . All right?

1 clock in and out
2 ask for permission to leave the premises
3 work irregular hours
4 do overtime
5 sleep in a hammock
6 man the switchboard at weekends
7 remember the combination of the safe
8 wear uniform
9 call the boss 'Sir'
10 stand up when the boss's wife comes in
11 carry a gun
12 patrol the premises at night
13 look after guard dogs
14 set burglar alarms
15 be responsible for security
16 suspect everyone
17 report anything suspicious
18 keep a copy of your reports
19 fill in forms in triplicate
20 take the blame if anything goes wrong

36 feel like + gerund

☐ PEG 97

One member of the family feels energetic; the other doesn't.

(a) A: Let's go for a walk.
   B: *I don't feel like going for a walk.* (slight stress on **feel**.)

This could also be used as an indirect speech exercise:

(b) A: Let's go for a walk.
   B (reporting A's suggestion): *He suggests/suggested going for a walk.*

Let's . . .

1 walk to the village.
2 take the dogs out.
3 climb the mountain.
4 run round the block.
5 carry the boxes upstairs.
6 play tennis.
7 swim across the river.
8 pick apples.
9 look for mushrooms.
10 move the piano.
11 tidy the cupboard.
12 roll the tennis court.
13 prune the roses.
14 saw up the dead tree.
15 sweep the stairs.
16 repaper the sitting-room.
17 weed the rose-beds.
18 paint the greenhouse.
19 make a bonfire.
20 rebuild the garage.

37 for + gerund (punish someone for/apologize for/get into trouble for)

☑ PEG 98, 259

Tom is at a boarding school. His father has just received his half term report and is reading it out to his wife.

A: Tom broke sixteen windows during his first week!
(a) B: *Well, I hope they punished him for breaking sixteen windows.*
(b) B: *Well, I hope he apologized for breaking sixteen windows.*
(c) B: *Poor Tom. I expect he got into trouble for breaking sixteen windows.*

(Other constructions: A very indulgent mother might say, *Oh, well, I expect they are used to boys breaking windows.* Or she might just express surprise (and even admiration) by **fancy/imagine** + gerund: *Fancy breaking sixteen windows!*)

Tom . . .

1 kicked a football through the greenhouse roof!
2 drove the headmaster's car into the village pond!
3 refused to wear uniform!
4 was rude to the school governors!
5 cut down the goal posts!
6 ploughed up the cricket pitch!
7 put an alligator in the swimming bath!
8 burnt down the gymnasium!
9 wrecked the assembly hall!
10 poured milk into the grand piano!
11 sold the school tape recorders!
12 cheated at exams!
13 carved his name on the school door!
14 rode his bicycle along the passages!
15 wrote things on the walls!
16 climbed in and out by the fire escape!
17 woke everyone up when he came in!
18 made bombs in the laboratory!
19 tried to start a riot!
20 brought the whole school out on strike!

38 have difficulty (in) + gerund

☐   PEG 259

A: Did you find the house quite easily?
B: *No, I had a lot of difficulty (in) finding the house.*

Did you . . . quite easily?

1 fit everything into your case (*Use* **my.**)
2 hire a caravan
3 start the car
4 read the map
5 cross the river
6 find a place to park
7 persuade them to let you camp (*Use* **me.**)
8 put up the tent
9 light the fire
10 keep warm
11 understand him
12 make yourself understood
13 explain what you wanted
14 arrange a loan
15 raise the money
16 cash your cheque
17 get a visa
18 renew your passport
19 obtain a permit
20 make ends meet

39 have difficulty in + gerund, find it easy + infinitive

☑   PEG 259

This is an exercise in both structures and should be done by students working in pairs.

(i) *Prompt*: open the windows

(a) A: *Do you have difficulty (in) opening the windows?*
(b) B: *No, I find it quite easy to open them.*
(c) B: *No, I find them quite easy to open.* (See note below.)

(ii) *Prompt*: deal with the correspondence

(a) A: *Do you have any difficulty in dealing with the correspondence?*
(b) B: *No, I find it quite easy to deal with it.*
(c) B: *No, I find it quite easy to deal with.* (See note below.)

Note: *I find it easy to open them/it* implies that the speaker has the necessary skill. *I find them/it easy to open* implies that it is easy to open them/it.

1–10 The hall porter of a block of flats is answering questions

1   regulate the central heating
2   organize the cleaning
3   control the cleaning staff
4   remember the tenants' names
5   answer telephone enquiries
6   deal with complaints
7   understand foreign tenants
8   operate the switchboard
9   read the meters
10   get on with the tenants

11–20 A farmer is answering questions

11   milk your cows
12   feed the calves
13   start your tractor
14   tow that big trailer
15   service your farm machinery
16   obtain spare parts
17   shear your sheep
18   train sheepdogs
19   obey all the regulations
20   sell your produce

39

40 it's no use/good + gerund
it's no use/good me/my + gerund

☐   PEG 261, 262

A: Why didn't you tell him?

(a) B: *It's no use telling him.*
or
B: *It's no good telling him.*

(b) B: *It's no use me/my telling him.* (normally with a slight stress on **me/my**)

(c) B: *It's no use me/my telling him, but if you told him something might be done.* (stress on **me/my** and **you**)

Why didn't you . . .

1   talk to him?
2   remind him?
3   ask him?
4   complain?
5   suggest a remedy?
6   make a fuss?
7   ring him?
8   refuse?
9   speak out?
10   threaten him?
11   offer a reward?
12   apply?
13   resign?
14   warn him?
15   sign?
16   strike?
17   go to the embassy?
18   demand compensation?
19   leave?
20   oppose him?

41 insist on + gerund, insist on me/my + gerund

☐ PEG 262

(a) A: Tom painted the ceiling black, didn't he?
B (in resigned tones): *Yes, he insisted on painting the ceiling black.*

(b) A: You painted the ceiling black, didn't you?
B: *Yes, Bill insisted on me/my painting the ceiling black. (Bill made me paint . . .* would also be possible.)

(a) *Tom . . . didn't he?*   (b) *You . . . didn't you?*

1   wore a tie,
2   changed trains,
3   started at midnight, ·
4   travelled in the guard's van,
5   post-dated the cheque,
6   sent for the Fire Brigade,
7   burnt the film,
8   took the dogs,
9   wrote to the papers,
10 slept in the attic,
11 consulted a fortune-teller,
12 pulled the communication cord,
13 fetched a doctor,
14 stopped the traffic,
15 searched the house,
16 rang the police,
17 defused the bomb,
18 marched in the procession,
19 waited till the end,
20 signed the petition,

42 in spite of + gerund

■ PEG 259, 329

Prompt: He spends very little.

A: He is quite rich.
B: *But in spite of being quite rich, he spends very little.*

The sentences could of course be joined by **although/though**.

Prompts are given in *italics*.

1 *He got the job*. He knows no Spanish.
2 *He got there first*. He started last.
3 *He remained sober*. He drank a lot.
4 *She arrived in time*. She missed the first train.
5 *They managed to cross the frontier*. They had no passports.
6 *He doesn't make much progress*. He practises a lot.
7 *She didn't lose any weight*. She dieted for six months.
8 *He never made enough to live on*. He worked hard.
9 *He never mastered the subject*. He studied for ten years.
10 *He didn't take good photographs*. He used very expensive cameras.
11 *She never looked smart*. She paid a lot for her clothes.
12 *She is always late for work*. She lives quite near the office.
13 *He passed his exams*. He did no work.
14 *It didn't sell well*. It was widely advertised.
15 *He was always looked on as a foreigner*. He spent his life in this country.

43 look forward to + gerund

☐ PEG 260B

A: When you get home you'll be able to ski, won't you?
B: *Yes, I'm looking forward to skiing.* (Leave objects unchanged.)

When you get home you'll be able to . . . won't you?

1 swim in the sea,
2 skate,
3 ride your horse again, (*Use* **my.**)
4 meet your friends, (*Use* **my.**)
5 speak your own language again, (*Use* **my.**)
6 drink wine,
7 fish in the river,
8 have a good holiday,
9 sunbathe,
10 show off your English, (*Use* **my.**)
11 take your dog for walks, (*Use* **my.**)
12 buy a lot of new clothes,
13 earn more money,
14 get a good job,
15 continue your university course, (*Use* **my.**)
16 start your training, (*Use* **my.**)
17 hear the local gossip,
18 go out without an umbrella,
19 open a language school,
20 write a book about your experiences, (*Use* **my.**)

44 make a point of + gerund

☐

A: She came late.
B: *Oh, she makes a point of coming late. She wants to attract attention.*

She . . .

1 arrived in a Rolls Royce.
2 parked the Rolls just outside the concert hall.
3 refused to queue at the box office.
4 argued about the prices.
5 insisted on seeing the manager.
6 kept everyone waiting.
7 smoked very powerful cigarettes.
8 used very strong scent.
9 wore most extraordinary clothes.
10 moved her seat several times.
11 fanned herself vigorously.
12 said she couldn't hear. (*Use* **can't.**)
13 clapped very loudly.
14 shouted 'Encore'.
15 drank double gins at the interval.
16 complained of the bad bar service.
17 contradicted the critics.
18 offered to write the reviews herself.
19 invited the soloists to dinner.
20 left before anyone else.

45 there's no point in + gerund, what's the point of + gerund

■ PEG 98A

A: The shops don't open till 9 but we'd better be there by 8.
(a) B: *But if the shops don't open till 9 there's no point in being there by 8.*
(b) B: *But if the shops don't open till 9 what's the point of being there by 8?*

1 The train doesn't leave till 9 but we'd better set out for the station at 7.
2 We aren't allowed to take photos but I'll bring my camera.
3 We can't park near the theatre but we'll take the car.
4 The pills aren't any good but we may as well finish the bottle.
5 We haven't any money but let's read the menus outside restaurants.
6 It's a job for men only but I'll advise Ann to apply for it.
7 None of the guests smoke but I'll provide them with ashtrays.
8 Tom hasn't a chance of getting elected but I'll vote for him.
9 Bill's plane doesn't land till 8 but we'd better be at the airport by 7.
10 I'm sure it's not going to rain but I'll take an umbrella.
11 They don't drink alcohol but I'll offer them gin.
12 It's too cold to bathe but pack a swimsuit.
13 My Alsation is quite harmless but I put up a notice saying, 'Beware of the dog'.
14 I know he'll refuse but I'll ask all the same. (*Omit* **all the same.**)
15 I don't want to buy anything but we may as well look round the shop.

46 succeed in + gerund, manage + infinitive

☑ PEG 241, 259

A: He reached the top in the end.
(a) B (surprised): *Oh, he succeeded in reaching it, did he?*
(b) B: *Oh, he managed to reach it, did he?*

He . . . in the end.

1 passed his driving test
2 finished the portrait
3 wrote his thesis
4 started the car
5 caught the plane
6 reached the finishing line
7 repaired the radio
8 got his visa
9 proved his innocence
10 solved the problem
11 climbed the mountain
12 grew a beard (*Use* **one.**)
13 fixed the aerial
14 found a house (*Use* **one.**)
15 recovered his property

47 hear + object + -ing

□, ▨ PEG 273

A noisy night.

A (tired and irritated): The dogs barked all night!

(a) B: *I didn't hear them barking.*

(b) B: *I heard them barking, but it didn't keep me awake.*

1 The wind whistled (all night)!
2 The dogs howled!
3 The windows rattled!
4 The stairs creaked!
5 The mice squeaked!
6 The rats ran about!
7 The tap dripped!
8 The pipes gurgled!
9 The church clock struck the quarters! (*Omit* **the quarters.**)
10 Water dripped through the ceiling! (*Omit* **the ceiling.**)
11 Thunder rumbled!
12 Chimneys crashed to the ground!
13 People in the street screamed!
14 Ambulance sirens wailed!
15 Traffic roared past!
16 The baby yelled!
17 Owls hooted!
18 Doors banged!
19 The man upstairs groaned!
20 My brother snored!

48 hear + object + -ing

☐ PEG 273

Bill is living in a room formerly occupied by Andrew. Andrew asks if the other tenants are as noisy as they were in his day. Apparently they are! The walls and floors in this house are very thin!

A: Does Miss Jones still type all night?
B: *Yes, I hear her typing.*

1 Does Mr Jones still sing in his bath?
2 Does Peter Jones still whistle as he goes downstairs?
3 Do the Smiths still quarrel?
4 Does the Jones baby still cry a lot?
5 Do Mr Brown's dogs still bark a lot?
6 Does Mrs Brown still cough when she goes down the stairs?
7 Does Mr White still walk about at night?
8 Do Mr and Mrs White still argue all the time?
9 Does Mr White's alarm clock still go off at six?
10 Does Mr White still swear when it goes off?
11 Does Mrs Smith still hoover every morning?
12 Does she still use her sewing machine every afternoon?
13 Do the Smith girls still tap-dance?
14 Does the Smith boy still practise the violin all night?
15 Do the other tenants complain about this?
16 Does Mrs Smith still nag at her husband?
17 Does Mr White still hammer on the walls?
18 Do the children still scream at each other?
19 Do they still run up and down the corridors?
20 Do they still bang on the doors as they pass? (*Keep* **on the doors.**)

49 hear + object + -ing
hear + object + infinitive without **to**

☐ PEG 273

A: Are you sure Tom left?
(a) B: *Yes, I heard him leaving.*
(b) B: *Yes, I heard him leave.*

A: Are you sure he told Ann?
(a) B: *Yes, I heard him telling her.*
(b) B: *Yes, I heard him tell her.*

Are you sure . . .

1 Tom booked the tickets?
2 Jack invited Mrs Jones?
3 Mrs Jones accepted the invitation?
4 Mary told her husband?
5 the lift doors shut?
6 Peter wound the clock?
7 the bell rang?
8 they accused Bill?
9 the bus stopped?
10 the ice cracked?
11 George spoke to Mary?
12 the passengers shouted at the driver?
13 the driver apologized?
14 Ann asked for the keys?
15 Peter complained about the delay?
16 the official explained?
17 Ann cancelled her reservation?
18 he threatened his students?
19 the students laughed?
20 they opened the champagne?

50 see + object + -ing

◢ PEG 273

A man visiting a foreign country expresses horror at what he sees. But his wife points out that he could see similar behaviour in their own country.

A: They push their way through!

B: *But you see people pushing their way through in our country too.*

They . . .

1 jump the queue!
2 drive much too fast!
3 ignore pedestrian crossings!
4 crash the lights!
5 double park!
6 elbow their way on to buses!
7 fight in the pubs!
8 sleep in the parks!
9 hang washing out of their windows!
10 go barefoot!
11 beg in the streets!
12 snatch purses!
13 play the guitar in the Underground!
14 dance in the streets!
15 run about nearly naked!
16 sit on the pavements!
17 write on the walls!
18 drop litter!
19 stare at foreigners!
20 cross the road without looking!

51 see + object + -ing, or see + object + infinitive without to

◪   PEG 273

A (with a note of doubt in his/her voice): Did he pay the bill?

(a) B: *Well, I didn't actually see him paying it.* (stress on **see**)
(b) B: *Well, I didn't actually see him pay it.* (stress on **see**)

Did he . . .

1   sign the cheque?
2   lock the door?
3   take the key?
4   read the instructions?
5   use the photocopier?
6   weigh the parcel?
7   post the letter?
8   burn the photographs?
9   copy the documents?
10 bury the gold?
11 throw the brick?
12 attack the postmistress?
13 give the injection?
14 sterilize the needle?
15 swallow the tablet?
16 oil the hinges?
17 drink the coffee?
18 cut the telephone cable?
19 open the safe?
20 take the money?

52 see/hear + object + -ing
see/hear + object + infinitive without to

☑ PEG 273

Bill was standing just outside the bank when the bank was raided.
A reporter is checking over his statement. The reporter speaks first:

A: You say that a white van pulled up?
(a) B: *Yes, I saw it pulling up.*
(b) B: *Yes, I saw it pull up.*

A: You say the raiders told the manager to open the safe?
(a) B: *Yes, I heard them telling him to open the safe.*
(b) B: *Yes, I heard them tell him to open the safe.*

Use **saw** or **heard**, whichever seems most logical.

You say that . . .

1 a white van stopped outside the bank?
2 four masked men leapt out?
3 they dashed into the bank?
4 one of them demanded the keys of the safe?
5 they smashed the grille?
6 a woman customer screamed?
7 the raiders shouted at her?
8 the alarm went off?
9 the police arrived?
10 the raiders rushed out of the bank?
11 they seized a woman as a hostage? (*Omit* **as a hostage**.)
12 they threatened to kill her?
13 they dragged her towards their car?
14 the police sergeant told them to release her?
15 the raiders fired at him?
16 the sergeant ordered his men to fire back?
17 passers-by ran for cover?
18 the leader of the raiders fell?
19 he lay bleeding on the ground?
20 the others surrendered?

53 see/hear + object + -ing

☑ PEG 273

Trouble with football fans.

A: A lot of their supporters behaved very badly. You saw them, didn't you?

B: *Well, I saw a few of them behaving very badly.* (Stress **few**)

A: A lot of them threatened the referee. You heard them, didn't you?

B: *Well, I heard a few of them threatening the referee.* (Stress **few**)

See also Drill 24.

A lot of . . . didn't you?

1 climbed over the wall. You saw them,
2 walked about on the grandstand roof. You saw them,
3 kicked our fans. You saw them,
4 made a horrible noise. You heard them,
5 threw bottles on to the ground. You saw them,
6 shouted insults at our team. You heard them,
7 screamed abuse at the referee. You heard them,
8 ran on to the field. You saw them,
9 attacked the referee. You saw them,
10 dug up the pitch. You saw them,
11 tried to pull down the goal posts. You saw them,
12 demanded a replay. You heard them,
13 overturned cars. You saw them,
14 smashed windows. You heard them,
15 drank whisky out of bottles. You saw them,
16 staggered about drunk. You saw them,
17 jostled the passers-by. You saw them,
18 stole fruit from the market. You saw them,
19 tried to climb the lamp-posts. You saw them,
20 splashed about in the fountains. You heard them,

54 spend + time + -ing

☐   PEG 275

A: Do you ever clean your flat?
B: *Yes. I spent all yesterday afternoon cleaning my flat.*

Do you ever . . .

1 tidy up?
2 put the books back on the shelves?
3 wash the coffee cups?
4 remove the empty bottles?
5 sweep up the broken glass?
6 empty the ashtrays?
7 hoover the carpets?
8 make the beds?
9 throw out the cracked cups?
10 replace the broken bulbs?
11 apologize to the landlord?
12 advise Bill to stop drinking?
13 tune the piano?
14 shake the mats?
15 take the dog for a walk?
16 pay your bills?
17 do your income tax returns?
18 wind the clocks?
19 weed your window box?
20 try to lose weight?

55 had better + infinitive without to
it's time + subject + past tense

◪ PEG 120, 293

Alan and Bill have got work abroad for a year and each is taking his car. They mean to leave together, but Bill is a bit behindhand with his preparations.

A: I've rung my parents.
(a) B: *Oh, I'd better ring my parents.* (stress on **my**)
(b) B: *Oh, I suppose it's time I rang my parents.* (stress on 'I' and **my**)

I've . . .

1 paid my bills.
2 said goodbye to my colleagues.
3 sub-let my flat.
4 told my landlord.
5 written to my new boss.
6 applied for my visa.
7 stopped my newspapers.
8 bought my maps.
9 worked out my route.
10 read my instructions.
11 had my injections.
12 collected my traveller's cheques.
13 insured my luggage.
14 arranged to have my mail forwarded.
15 put on my roof rack.
16 adjusted my brakes.
17 tested my lights.
18 checked my tyres.
19 changed my money.
20 done my packing.

56 let + object + infinitive without **to**

☑ PEG 246D

(a) A: He wanted to go but I said 'No'.
   B: *But why didn't you let him go?* (slight stress on **didn't**)

Alternatively the first sentence could be in the form:

(b) A: He would have gone if I'd let him.
   B: *But why didn't you let him go?*
   or
(c) B: *Why on earth didn't you let him go?*

Leave noun objects unchanged.

(a) *He wanted to . . . but I said 'No'.*	(b) and (c) *He would have . . . if I'd let him.*
1 stop	1 stopped
2 help	2 helped
3 pay	3 paid
4 hitch-hike	4 hitch-hiked
5 lead the way	5 led the way
6 take a short cut	6 taken a short cut
7 tell the truth	7 told the truth
8 give evidence	8 given evidence
9 leave early	9 left early
10 tell you about it (*Use* **me**.)	10 told you about it
11 phone his brother	11 phoned his brother
12 decide for himself	12 decided for himself
13 join the club	13 joined the club
14 use his real name	14 used his real name
15 bring his passport	15 brought his passport
16 mark the cards	16 marked the cards
17 finish the bottle	17 finished the bottle
18 smoke a cigar	18 smoked a cigar
19 drive home	19 driven home
20 wear a kilt	20 worn a kilt

57 let + object + infinitive without to, be allowed + infinitive

☐ PEG 130, 246D

The Smiths and their two boys and the Browns and their two girls went to the same holiday resort but at different times. Afterwards the boys and girls compared notes. The boys had a much more interesting time! The boys speak first.

(a) Active:

A: We went rock climbing.
B: *Our parents wouldn't let us go rock-climbing.* (stress on **our** and **let**)

(b) Passive:

A: We ran about without shoes.
B: *We weren't allowed to run about without shoes.* (stress on **we** and **allowed**)

We weren't let run about . . . is also possible but much less usual than *We weren't allowed to* . . .

Keep nouns unchanged.

We . . .

1 ran about without shoes.
2 slept in the garden.
3 practised parachuting.
4 played water polo.
5 sailed round the island.
6 water-skied.
7 had bicycle races on the sand.
8 canoed down the river.
9 climbed the cliffs.
10 went surfing.
11 rode Peter's pony.
12 dived off the pier.
13 explored the caves.
14 learnt how to scuba-dive.
15 took lessons in hang-gliding.

58 let + object + infinitive without to, be allowed + infinitive

☐   PEG 130, 246D

Ann's son is extremely troublesome. Ann's friend thinks that this is partly Ann's fault.

(a) A: He bullies his sisters.
     B: *But why do you let him bully his sisters?*

Put the first sentence in the past tense:

(b) A: He bullied his sisters.
     B: *Why did you let him bully his sisters?* (stress on **let**)

(c) A: He bullied his sisters.
     B: *He shouldn't have been allowed to bully his sisters.* (stress on **allowed**)

(d) A: He bullied his sisters.
     B: *Why was he allowed to bully his sisters?* (stress on **allowed**)

For drills (b) (c) and (d) use the sentences in (a) with the verbs in the past tense. Leave nouns unchanged.

He . . .

1 kicks his brother.
2 shouts at his sisters.
3 fights with the neighbours' children.
4 upsets everyone.
5 answers back.
6 disobeys me. (*Use* **you**.)
7 breaks the furniture.
8 steals from my purse. (*Use* **your**.)
9 misses school every Monday.
10 watches TV all Saturday.
11 plays his radio till 2 a.m.
12 stays in bed all Sunday.
13 comes down late for breakfast.
14 puts his elbows on the table.
15 talks with his mouth full.
16 takes more than his share.
17 rides his bicycle along the pavements.
18 roller-skates up and down the corridors.
19 uses awful language.
20 reads terrible comics.

59 **make** + object + infinitive without **to**

◪ PEG 246E

(a) A: He told Ann, I hope.
  B: *Yes, I made him tell her.*

(b) He put on his gloves, I hope.
  Yes, I made him put them on.
  (Notice word order.)

(a) *He . . . I hope.*

1 apologized
2 explained
3 paid the bill
4 wrote to the Smiths
5 cleaned the bath
6 took his medicine
7 reported the accident
8 waited for Ann
9 rang his parents
10 finished the book
11 answered the letter
12 made his bed
13 cleaned his shoes
14 changed his socks
15 wore his best suit
16 moved his car
17 insured his house
18 fastened his safety belt
19 did his exercises
20 checked the tyre pressures

(b) *He . . . I hope.*

1 hung up his coat
2 turned down the radio
3 shaved off his beard
4 took back the books
5 picked up the pieces
6 kept on his coat
7 took down the notice
8 rolled up the carpet
9 locked up the papers
10 threw away his old boots
11 filled up the form
12 looked up the time of the train
13 switched off the central heating
14 paid back the money
15 put away his tools

60 make + object + infinitive without to
be made + infinitive with to

☑ PEG 246E

Ann was temporarily in charge of a group of children, who were supposed to co-operate by looking after themselves and giving a hand with the housework. Mary doesn't think Ann was strict enough.

(a) Active
   A: Some of them ate their suppers. (slight stress on **some**)
   B: *You should have made them all eat their suppers.* (stress on **all**)

(b) Passive
   A: The girls ate their suppers. (stress on **girls**)
   B: *The boys should have been made to eat their suppers too.*

(a) *Some of them . . .*	(b) *The girls . . .*
1 drank milk.	1 drank milk.
2 washed their faces.	2 washed their faces.
3 brushed their hair.	3 brushed their hair.
4 cleaned their teeth.	*etc., as in* (a)
5 put away their toys.	
6 helped with the washing up.	
7 did some housework.	
8 wrote to their parents.	
9 swept their rooms.	
10 wiped their boots.	
11 hung up their clothes.	
12 said 'Please'.	
13 ate their breakfast.	
14 ran round the football field.	
15 slept with their windows open.	
16 got up early.	
17 had a cold bath every morning.	
18 went to bed early.	
19 swept under their beds.	
20 picked blackberries.	

61 happen + present and continuous infinitives

■   PEG 241A, G

The first speaker is very suspicious.

A: You asked him the time. Was this part of a plan?
B: *No, I just happened to ask him the time.*

A: You were looking out of the window when I passed. Was this part of
a plan?
B: *No, I just happened to be looking out of the window.*

Both types will be found in the following exercise. If a simple tense is
used as in the first example, use the present infinitive. If a continuous
tense is used, as in the second example, use the continuous infinitive.

You . . .

1 were in the phone box when I passed. Were you watching me?
2 looked at your watch. Was this a signal of some kind?
3 were sitting by the window when I passed. Were you watching me?
4 were leaning against your gate when I passed. Were you watching me?
5 winked at Tom. Was this a signal of some kind?
6 were waiting for a bus when I passed. Were you watching me?
7 gave him a lift. Was this part of a plan?
8 were standing in your doorway when I passed. Were you watching me?
9 travelled on the same train as Peter. Was this part of a plan?
10 were watering your window-box when I passed. Were you watching
me?
11 got out at the same station as Peter. Was this part of a plan?
12 had your tape recorder with you. Was this part of a plan?
13 waved at Jack. Was this a signal?
14 were painting your railings when I passed. Were you watching me?
15 sat at the same table as Jack. Was this part of a plan?
16 were clipping your hedge when I passed. Were you watching me?
17 put up your umbrella when you saw Bill. Was this a signal?
18 were wearing dark glasses when I saw you. Was this part of a plan?
19 and Peter exchanged briefcases. Was this intentional?
20 were looking through your binoculars when I passed. Were you
watching me?

62 mean + infinitive

☐ PEG 114, 269B

A: I suppose you did a lot of cycling.

(a) B: *Well, I meant to do a lot of cycling but the weather wasn't suitable.* (slight stress on **meant**)

(b) B: *Well, we were meant to do a lot of cycling but the weather wasn't suitable.* (slight stress on **meant**)

suppose could be used for **mean** in (b), but not in (a): *We were supposed to do a lot of cycling.*

Note that the situation in (b) is different from the situations in (a). In (a) Bill went on holiday alone and made his own plans. In (b) he joined a group where activities were planned by the organizers. Note also that in (a) **meant** means **intended** but that in (b) **meant** could also convey an idea of duty.

(c) *I was to have done/We were to have done* . . . could be used for both (a) and (b). But there is no indication of duty here. This form merely expresses an unfulfilled plan.

I suppose you . . .

1 swam before breakfast.
2 went pony-trekking.
3 dug ditches.
4 watched birds.
5 looked for rare plants.
6 picked strawberries.
7 took aerial photographs.
8 made sketch maps of the area.
9 painted landscapes.
10 walked a lot.
11 climbed the mountains.
12 spent all day in the open.
13 examined the rocks.
14 collected rock specimens.
15 slept in tents.
16 cooked in the open.
17 hunted for fossils.
18 studied the wild life in the area.
19 planted trees.
20 followed the river to its source.

63 occur + to + object + infinitive

☐   PEG 241B

A: I hope you gave Tom a drink.
B: *No, it never occurred to me to give him a drink.* (= I never thought of it.)

I hope you . . .

1 invited Ann.
2 offered Tom a drink.
3 wrote to Mrs Smith.
4 thanked the twins.
5 made Bill some coffee.
6 put George up for the night.
7 rang Andrew.
8 said 'Hello'.
9 congratulated Margaret.
10 apologized to James.
11 kept Mary a place.
12 told the children a story.
13 waited for Peter.
14 sent James a present.
15 helped the girls with their luggage.
16 showed Susan the way.
17 gave Bob a lift.
18 saw Alice home.
19 wished Bill luck.
20 kissed Hilda.

64 offer + infinitive

☐ PEG 241A

A: Peter paid for me.
B: *He offered to pay for me too, but I refused.* (stress on **me** and **too**)

A: Peter painted my door.
B: *He offered to paint my door too, but I refused.* (stress on **my** and **too**)
or
B: *He offered to paint mine too, but I refused.* (stress on **mine** and **too**)

Peter . . .

1 waited for me.
2 gave me a lift.
3 lent me £5.
4 found me a job.
5 got me a seat.
6 showed me the way.
7 washed my car.
8 helped me.
9 carried my luggage.
10 saw me off.
11 met my train.
12 stood me a drink.
13 tuned my guitar.
14 drove me home.
15 put me up.
16 looked after my dog.
17 typed my essay.
18 dug my garden.
19 repaired my washing machine.
20 fixed my TV.

65 remember/forget + infinitive

PEG 268

Ann's bad memory saves her a lot of trouble.

(a) A: I locked the safe. Ann had forgotten.
    B: *Oh, Ann never remembers to lock it.*
    or
    B: *Oh, Ann always forgets to lock it.*

(b) A: I took down the old notices. Ann had forgotten.
    B: *Oh, Ann never remembers to take them down.*
    or
    B: *Oh, Ann always forgets to take them down.* (Notice word order.)

I . . . Ann had forgotten.

1 turned out the lights. (*See* (b) *above.*)
2 switched off the TV. (*See* (b) *above.*)
3 shut the lift doors.
4 paid the milkman.
5 took the milk in. (*See* (b) *above.*)
6 washed the coffee cups.
7 made coffee.
8 swept the floor.
9 dusted the desks.
10 put up the new notices. (*See* (b) *above.*)
11 watered the pot plants.
12 thanked the office cleaners.
13 put out the rubbish. (*See* (b) *above.*)
14 stamped the letters.
15 checked the petty cash.
16 bought the biscuits.
17 fed the tropical fish. (*Use* **them.**)
18 covered the typewriters.
19 set the burglar alarm.
20 locked the office.

66 seem + infinitive

□   PEG 241

Mr X has recently come to live in the area, but seems to wish to avoid people. This of course arouses interest and his neighbours observe him closely. Two of them are talking about him. The first speaker makes confident assertions; the second is more cautious.

A: He wishes to avoid us.
B: *Well, he seems to wish to avoid us.* (slight stress on **seems**)

He . . .

1 is afraid of someone.
2 suspects everyone.
3 distrusts his neighbours.
4 dislikes children.
5 likes dogs.
6 avoids people.
7 reads a lot.
8 prefers to be alone.
9 thinks he is in danger.
10 lives on pills.
11 eats very little.
12 feeds his dogs well.*
13 drinks a good deal.
14 writes a lot of letters.
15 works at night.
16 has plenty of money.
17 knows several languages.
18 takes a lot of photos.
19 develops his own films.
20 believes in ghosts.

67 seem + continuous infinitive

☑ PEG 241G

Two people keep a close eye on Mr Smith, who lives opposite. The road is wide and busy so they do not see exactly what is happening, but they have a general idea.

A: He doesn't usually watch television.
B: *Well, he seems to be watching it today.*

A: He doesn't usually get letters.
B: *Well, he seems to be getting some today.*

He doesn't usually . . .

1 talk to his mother-in-law.
2 help his wife.
3 use the public phone box.
4 try to please his wife.
5 wear a suit. (*Use* **one**.)
6 play with the children.
7 bring his wife flowers.
8 take photographs.
9 do the shopping.
10 carry his wife's parcels.
11 leave the car at home.
12 let his wife drive.
13 quarrel with his neighbours.
14 shout at his neighbour's dogs.
15 walk to work.
16 pay cash.
17 collect the children from school.
18 read the paper.
19 wait for his wife.
20 shake his fist at us.

68 seem/appear/is said/is supposed + perfect infinitive

■ PEG 255C

Two people are visiting a 'stately home' built in the eighteenth century by a famous duke. One asks questions about the duke, which the other, who has just bought the guide book, does his best to answer.

   A: Was he rich? (**very**)
(a) B: *Yes, he seems to have been very rich.*
(b) B: *Yes, he appears to have been very rich.*
(c) B: *Yes, he is said to have been very rich.*
(d) B: *Yes, he is supposed to have been very rich.*

   1 Did he live here? (**most of his life**)
   2 Did he marry? (**several times**)
   3 Did he have children? (**a lot of**)
   4 Did he build any other houses? (**several**)
   5 Did he own (large) estates? (**enormous**)
   6 Did he employ a (large) staff? (**huge**)
   7 Was he a (good) landlord? (**excellent**)
   8 Did his tenants like him? (**very much**)
   9 Did he entertain? (**lavishly**)
  10 Did he drink? (**heavily**)
  11 Did he hunt? (**when he was a young man**)
  12 Did he keep racehorses? (**all his life**)
  13 Did they win races? (**quite a lot of**)
  14 Did he lose money gambling? (**a fortune**)
  15 Did he sell his other houses? (**two of them**)
  16 Did he quarrel with his neighbours? (**some of them**)
  17 Did he fight duels? (**two**)
  18 Did he kill his opponent? (**both times**)
  19 Did he leave the country? (**after the second duel**)
  20 Did he die (abroad)? (**in Paris**)

69 subject + **used** + infinitive

□ PEG 162B

A: Do you swim?
B: *No, I used to swim a lot but I don't now.*

Do you . . .

1 smoke?
2 drink?
3 garden?
4 eat out?
5 read?
6 write?
7 sing?
8 gossip?
9 gamble?
10 travel?
11 ride?
12 paint?
13 sail?
14 dream?
15 listen to the radio? (Omit **to the radio.**)
16 go (to concerts)?
17 play tennis? (Omit **tennis.**)
18 argue with your husband? (Use **him.**)
19 quarrel with your mother-in-law? (Use **her.**)
20 complain?

70 subject + **used** + infinitive

☑ PEG 162B

A: Peter is sweeping his room.
B: *Is he? I used to sweep my room too, but I don't now.*

A: Peter has just paid his telephone bill.
B: *Has he? I used to pay my telephone bill too, but I don't now.*

Use the appropriate auxiliary for the first phrase. Stress 'I' and 'my'.

Peter . . .

1 is washing up.
2 has just shaved.
3 goes to evening classes.
4 cuts his toenails.
5 washes his socks.
6 reads the newspaper.
7 took back his library books.
8 is emptying his ashtrays.
9 is sewing on buttons.
10 has polished his shoes.
11 wears a tie.
12 sweeps his floor.
13 goes to work.
14 got up early.
15 writes to the newspapers.
16 gives advice to his children.
17 is saving money.
18 has made his bed.
19 stamps his letters.
20 cleans the bath.

71 be afraid + infinitive

☐ PEG 271A

(a) Bill explains why he did not act as Alan expected.

A: You went on, I suppose.
B: *No, I was afraid to go on.*

A: You gave the injection, I suppose.
B: *No, I was afraid to give it.*

(b) Alternative answers are *No, I didn't dare to go on/give it* and *No, I dared not go on/give it.*

Compare with Drill 33, *be afraid of.*

You . . . I suppose.

1 jumped out,
2 climbed down,
3 used the lift,
4 complained,
5 drank the coffee,
6 interrupted him,
7 contradicted him,
8 mentioned it to your wife,
9 told your colleagues,
10 informed the police,
11 opened the packet,
12 went out at night, (*Keep* **night.**)
13 said something, (*Use* **anything.**)
14 appealed,
15 answered the phone,

72 be + horrified/glad/surprised/amazed/relieved etc. + infinitive

☑ PEG 26F

A: I saw smoke coming under the door. (horrified)
B: *I was horrified to see smoke coming under the door.*

(This is just an exercise, not a conversation.)

1 I heard cries of pain coming from the next room. (horrified)
2 I saw a photograph of myself on the front page. (astonished)
3 I found a complete stranger taking food out of my fridge. (annoyed)
4 I saw that the beds had been made. (glad)
5 I received an invitation to the palace. (delighted)
6 I found that no preparations had been made. (surprised)
7 I heard that the last train had just left. (dismayed)
8 I found everyone still in bed at eleven o'clock. (shocked)
9 I saw blood all over the carpet. (appalled)
10 I heard rats running up and down inside the walls. (amazed)
11 I found the last bus still standing there. (relieved)
12 I heard that you can't come ski-ing after all. (disappointed)
13 I learnt that no room had been reserved for me. (annoyed)
14 I saw that most of the town had been destroyed by the explosion. (appalled)
15 I heard that my brother's plane had crashed. (horrified)
16 I heard that my brother was safe. (relieved)
17 I found that I could make myself understood. (pleased)
18 I saw that I had passed the exam. (glad)
19 I found my name at the very bottom of the list. (sorry)
20 I heard that I could have every weekend off. (delighted)

73 it is/was + adjective + of + object + infinitive

□ PEG 26B1

A: He warned me. (**kind**)
B: *It was kind of him to warn you.*

1 They waited for me. (**good**)
2 He lent Ann his bicycle. (**kind**)
3 She believed him. (**stupid**)
4 They invited me. (**nice**)
5 She told the police. (**sensible**)
6 I found the way. (**clever**) (*Use* **you**.)
7 She left her car unlocked. (**careless**)
8 He had another drink. (**rash**)
9 He asked Bill to drive. (**prudent**)
10 She argued with the customs officer. (**idiotic**)
11 He refused to share his sandwiches. (**selfish**)
12 They ran away. (**cowardly**)
13 He kept the money. (**dishonest**)
14 He took the only cream cake. (**greedy**)
15 She jumped into the river to save the child. (**brave**)
16 He offered to pay. (**generous**)
17 He suggested going Dutch. (**mean**)
18 He said I wasn't any use. (**unkind**)
19 He told lies about me. (**wicked**)
20 He admitted he was wrong. (**courageous**)

74 what a/an + adjective + noun + infinitive

☐   PEG 26B2

A: He sleeps in a wine cellar. (**odd place**)
B: *What an odd place to sleep!*

He . . .

1   lives in a cave. (**funny place**)
2   is studying dowsing. (**odd thing**)
3   parked outside the police station. (**silly place**)
4   travels by donkey. (**slow way**)
5   said, 'Mind your own business.' (**rude thing**)
6   sleeps in his car. (**uncomfortable place**)
7   makes money by telling fortunes. (**interesting way**)
8   swims at night. (**odd time**)
9   plays golf on his flat roof. (**strange place**)
10   makes all his important decisions in the lift. (**extraordinary place**)
11   lives on brown rice. (**odd thing**) (*Keep* **on.**)
12   cooks in his bathroom. (**queer place**)
13   rings up friends at 6 a.m. (**inconvenient time**)
14   keeps (his) money in an old sock. (**unsafe place**)
15   spends his free time at the railway station. (**noisy place**) (*Use* **one's** *for* **his.**)
16   relaxes by standing on his head. (**odd way**)
17   reads the telephone directory. (**strange thing**)
18   gets up at 4 a.m. (**unpleasant time**)
19   has a holiday in June. (**agreeable time**)
20   drives a Rolls Royce. (**expensive car**)

75 too + adjective + infinitive, adjective + enough + infinitive

☐ PEG 252A,B

A: Bob got another job, I suppose? (old/young)
(a) B: *No, he was too old to get another job.*
(b) B: *Yes, he was young enough to get another job.*

. . . I suppose?

1 Tom went alone, (**young/old**)
2 Peter got through the window, (**fat/thin**)
3 George drove the car, (**drunk/sober**)
4 Ann waited quietly, (**impatient/patient**)
5 Mary walked upstairs, (**weak/strong**)
6 Peter ate something, (**ill/well**) (*Use* **anything** with **ill, something** with **well.**)
7 James bought the house, (**poor/rich**)
8 Frank understood, (**stupid/clever**)
9 Bill rode the pony, (**heavy/light**)
10 The other driver listened to you, (**excited/calm**)
11 She wore your fur coat, (**short/tall**)
12 Jack became a jockey, (**big/small**)
13 Mary applied again, (**discouraged/optimistic**)
14 Oliver tried the new system, (**unenterprising/enterprising**)
15 Your boss gives you a bonus, (**mean/generous**) (*Use* **us.**)
16 Tom admitted his mistake, (**proud/honest**)
17 Your grandmother wore jeans, (**conventional/unconventional**)
18 You lent Bill money, (**cautious/rash**)
19 James sympathized with the younger generation, (**narrow-minded/broad-minded**)
20 He said that it was your fault, (**polite/impolite**)

76 too + adjective + infinitive, adjective + enough + infinitive

☑ PEG 252A,B

A: You carried the case? (**heavy/light**)

(a) B: *No, it was too heavy to carry.*
   or
   No, it was too heavy for me to carry.

(b) B: *Yes, it was light enough to carry.*
   or
   Yes, it was light enough for me to carry.

A: You put the boat on the roof rack? (**big/small**)

(a) B: *No, it was too big to put on the roof rack.*

(b) B: *Yes, it was small enough to put on the roof rack.*

for me/you/him etc. is not necessary except when it is important to emphasize who is doing the action.

You . . .

1 ate the apple? (**sour/sweet**)
2 grilled the steak? (**tough/tender**)
3 pushed the packet under the door? (**thick/thin**)
4 read the inscription? (**faint/clear**)
5 saw the bird's nest quite clearly? (**high/low**)
6 put the trunk in the boot of the car? (**big/small**)
7 towed the boat behind the car? (**heavy/light**)
8 put your umbrella in your suitcase? (**long/short**)
9 waded across the river? (**deep/shallow**)
10 jumped across the stream? (**wide/narrow**)
11 picked the fruit? (**unripe/ripe**)
12 sent it by post? (**fragile/sturdy**)
13 used yesterday's milk? (**sour/fresh**)
14 drank the coffee? (**hot/cool**)
15 wore your blue suit? (**shabby/smart**)

77 too + adjective + infinitive, adjective + enough + infinitive

▣ PEG 252A,B

A: You sat on the grass, I suppose? (**wet/dry**)
(a) A: *No, it was too wet to sit on.*
     or
     No, it was too wet for us to sit on.
(b) B: *Yes, it was dry enough to sit on.*
     or
     Yes, it was dry enough for us to sit on.

A: The plane landed on the field, I suppose? (**rough/smooth**)
(a) B: *No, it was too rough to land on.*
     or
     No, it was smooth enough to land on.
(b) B: *Yes, it was smooth enough to land on.*
     or
     Yes, it was smooth enough for the plane to land on.

   . . . I suppose?

1 You slept in the cave, (**wet/dry**)
2 They camped on the ledge, (**narrow/wide**)
3 He walked on the ice, (**thin/thick**)
4 He slid down the pole, (**rough/smooth**)
5 The plane landed on the sand, (**soft/hard**)
6 You took out the (electric light) bulb, (**hot/cool**)
7 She read by the light of the moon, (**dim/bright**)
8 You saw through the hedge, (**thick/thin**)
9 He dived from the pier, (**high/low**)
10 She handed in her exercise, (**untidy/tidy**)
11 You swam in the river, (**polluted/clean**)
12 He stood on the table, (**unsteady/steady**)
13 She dived into the pond, (**shallow/deep**)
14 You sat on the floor, (**dirty/clean**)
15 You picked up the sack of potatoes, (**heavy/light**)

78 Purpose expressed by the infinitive

□   PEG 334A

A: He learnt to cook in Paris. Were you surprised?
B: *No. He went to Paris to learn to cook.* (slight stress on **went**)
   or
B: *No. He went to Paris in order to learn to cook.* (slight stress on **order**)

He . . . Were you surprised?

1 arranged a loan in Zurich.
2 met Bill in Edinburgh.
3 sold his pictures in London.
4 opened a bank account in Switzerland.
5 painted a portrait in Florence.
6 learnt to fly in Australia.
7 played tennis in Florida.
8 bought diamonds in Amsterdam.
9 climbed mountains in Wales.
10 skied in Norway.
11 watched the penguins in the Antarctic.
12 dived for treasure in the Mediterranean.
13 had an eye operation in Barcelona.
14 gambled in Monte Carlo.
15 gave a concert in Munich.
16 studied judo in Japan.
17 visited the Spanish Riding School in Vienna.
18 wrote a book in Seville.
19 fished for salmon in Scotland.
20 photographed lions in Africa.

79 Purpose: **so as not** + infinitive

☑ PEG 334B

Tom has taken a room in a boarding house. The landlady has an old resident she particularly doesn't want to offend, so she gives Tom a list of things not to do.

A: You mustn't make a noise at night. It wakes Mrs Jones.
B: *All right. I won't make a noise at night so as not to wake Mrs Jones.*

You must not . . . Mrs Jones.

1 talk about traffic accidents. It frightens
2 criticize lady drivers. It offends
3 play the radio loudly. It disturbs
4 tell dirty jokes. It shocks
5 make a noise at night. It wakes
6 chew gum. It disgusts
7 bang doors. It startles
8 say anything about rising prices. It depresses
9 whistle. It irritates
10 discuss hijacking. It worries
11 sing in your bath. It annoys
12 smoke at meals. It upsets
13 come in late. It bothers
14 leave your bicycle in the hall. It inconveniences
15 mention illness. It distresses

80 Purpose clauses and **prevent** + object + gerund

■ PEG 336C

Ann has left her husband and is giving her solicitor her reasons for doing so. The solicitor repeats her complaints as he writes them down.

(a) A: He didn't like me going through his private papers so he locked them up.

B: *I see. He locked up his private papers so that you couldn't/wouldn't be able to go through them.*

(b) A: He didn't like me going through his private papers so he locked them up.

B: *I see. He locked up his private papers to prevent you going through them.*

(a) *He didn't like me . . .*

1 driving the car, so he took the keys to the office every day.
2 drinking during the day, so he locked the drinks cupboard.
3 drawing cheques, so he closed my account.
4 smoking his cigars, so he hid his cigar box.
5 going out after dark, so he locked the door.
6 watching television, so he sold the TV set.
7 opening bottles of wine, so he kept the corkscrew in his pocket.
8 borrowing his sweaters, so he locked the wardrobe.
9 ringing my friends late at night, so he disconnected the phone.
10 serving tinned soup, so he threw away the tin-opener.
11 taking money from the safe, so he changed the combination.
12 using his tools, so he locked his toolbox.
13 typing on his typewriter, so he removed the ribbon.
14 riding his bicycle, so he took a wheel off.
15 getting on the roof, so he put bars in the skylight.

(c) as in (b), but use an infinitive in each case, as this provides a better contrast with the ground:

He didn't like me to drive/drink/draw/smoke/go/watch/open/borrow/ring/serve/take/use/type/ride/get.

81 Purpose clauses: **so that** + subject + **would**

■ PEG 336A

The first speaker is very naïve.
A: He happened to be standing by his gate. So he saw the shooting.
B: *It was no accident. He was standing by his gate so that he would see the shooting.* (stress on **would**.)

1 He happened to leave his clothes on the beach. So we thought he was drowned.
2 She happened to put the letter on top of the pile. So he opened it first.
3 She accidently burnt the document. So we have no record of the agreement.
4 He happened to be wearing dark glasses. So no one recognized him.
5 He happened to be sitting on the letter. So we didn't see it.
6 By accident she gave us the wrong address. So we went to the wrong place.
7 She happened to mention Tom's name. So Tom was suspected.
8 He happened to be standing outside the door. So he heard the conversation.
9 They happened to be speaking French. So neither of us understood them.
10 They accidentally left a bicycle in the passage and Tom fell over it.
11 She happened to have left her umbrella at home. So she had to share Peter's.
12 He happened to post all his cards in Rome. So we assumed he spent his whole holiday there.
13 He happened to be in the telephone box. So he saw everything.
14 She happened to drop the report on Peter's desk. So Peter read it.
15 She accidentally dropped her handkerchief. Jack picked it up.

82 Purpose: in case

☑ PEG 337A

An over-protective mother gives instructions to her au pair girl.

A: If he bathes he'll catch cold.

(a) B: *I see. I'm not to let him bathe in case he catches cold.*

The au pair girl reports this conversation later.

(b) B: *I wasn't allowed to let him bathe in case he caught cold.*
   or
(c) B: *She told me not to let him bathe in case he caught cold.*

If he . . .

1 climbs trees he'll tear his trousers.
2 plays near the river he'll fall in.
3 talks to the neighbour's children he'll learn bad language.
4 runs about in the garden he'll trample the flowers.
5 strikes matches he'll burn himself.
6 uses the scissors he'll cut himself.
7 stands on his head he'll make himself giddy.
8 pats the dogs they will bite him.
9 strokes the cats they will scratch him.
10 shouts he'll disturb his grandfather.
11 kicks his football in the garden he'll damage the roses.
12 sits on the grass he'll catch a cold.
13 crosses the road alone he'll be run over.
14 goes out alone he'll lose his way.
15 carries a tray he'll drop it.
16 flies his kite he'll lose it.
17 sails his boat he'll get his feet wet.
18 throws his ball he'll break a window.
19 helps the painters he'll spill the paint.
20 rides his bicycle he'll have an accident.

83 might/shouldn't + perfect infinitive

■ PEG 133A, 143

This is a continuation of the previous exercise. The au pair girl, feeling sorry for the boy, allowed him to climb trees, kick his football etc., and the disasters predicted by his mother didn't happen. She tells the mother this.

A: He bathed and didn't catch cold.
B: *But you shouldn't have let him bathe! He might have caught cold.*

Alternatively:

A: He bathed.
B: *But you shouldn't have let him bathe!*

A: He didn't catch cold.
B: *But he might have caught cold!*

He . . .

1 climbed trees and didn't tear his trousers.
2 played near the river and didn't fall in.
3 talked to the neighbour's children and didn't learn bad language.
4 ran about in the garden and didn't trample the flowers.
5 struck matches and didn't burn himself.
6 used the scissors and didn't cut himself.
7 stood on his head and didn't make himself giddy.
8 patted the dogs and they didn't bite him.
9 stroked the cats and they didn't scratch him.
10 shouted and didn't disturb his grandfather.
11 kicked his football and didn't damage the roses.
12 sat on the grass and didn't catch a cold.
13 crossed the road and wasn't run over.
14 went out alone and didn't lose his way.
15 carried a tray and didn't drop it.
16 flew his kite and didn't lose it.
17 sailed his boat and didn't get his feet wet.
18 threw his ball and didn't break a window.
19 helped the painters and didn't spill the paint.
20 rode his bicycle and didn't have an accident.

84 Passive: simple present, simple past, present perfect and should

☑ PEG 302D, 303A

    A: In my college the domestic staff sweep the classrooms.
(a) B: *Our classrooms are swept by students.* (stress on **our**)
(b) B: *Our classrooms were swept by students.* (stress on **our**)
(c) B: *Our classrooms have always been swept by students.* (stress on **our**)
(d) B: *Our classrooms should be swept by students.* (stress on **students**)

In my college . . .

1 technicians service the equipment.
2 the schoolkeeper cleans the blackboards.
3 a cleaner keeps the common room tidy.
4 the catering staff cook the lunches.
5 the schoolkeeper rings the bells.
6 the cleaners empty the wastepaper baskets.
7 trained telephonists man the switchboard.
8 the maintenance staff replace broken windows.
9 a trained driver drives the college bus.
10 qualified librarians look after the library.
11 the welfare officer organizes the annual dance.
12 the music staff produce the annual concert.
13 the physical training instructor runs the sports club.
14 the entertainments officer arranges trips.
15 the college secretary collects the fees.
16 the Director draws up the year's programme.
17 a printing firm prints our college magazine.
18 a paid handyman does all our repairs.
19 the Governors choose the Principal.
20 the Principal appoints staff.

85 Passive: present continuous and past continuous

☑ PEG 302C

(a) A: They are widening our road.

B: *Oh, our road is being widened too.* (stress on **our**)

Later, a third person asks:

(b) A: *What did Bill say about the road?*

and is answered in indirect speech:

B: *He said it was being widened.*

They are . . .

1 repainting our bridge.
2 repairing our road.
3 widening our pavements.
4 changing our house numbers.
5 rebuilding our town hall.
6 taking down our park railings.
7 re-opening our theatre.
8 cleaning our statues.
9 closing down our local hospital.
10 moving our library.
11 replacing our street lights.
12 extending our no-traffic area.
13 re-routing our buses.
14 turning our local cinema into a Bingo hall.
15 making our street one-way.
16 resurfacing our road.
17 restoring our old church.
18 dredging our river.
19 demolishing our old library.
20 putting up our rates.

86 Passive: present perfect and past perfect

◪ PEG 303A

(a) A: Shall I buy the bread?
     B: *It's just been bought, actually.*

(b) A: Did you buy the bread?
     B: *No, when I arrived it had just been bought.*

(a) *Shall I . . .*

1 make the mayonnaise?
2 lay the table?
3 open the bottles?
4 grind the coffee?
5 fry the sausages?
6 wash the glasses?
7 whip the cream?
8 grate the cheese?
9 slice the cucumber?
10 boil the eggs?
11 shell the peas?
12 carve the chicken?
13 skin the tomatoes?
14 mix the salad dressing?
15 mash the potatoes?
16 core the apples?
17 peel the grapes?
18 squeeze the lemons?
19 grill the steak?
20 roast the chestnuts?

(b) *Did you . . .*

1 make the mayonnaise?
2 lay the table?
etc.

87 Passive: **may/might** + perfect infinitive

Ann and Bill are worried about a packet they are expecting from a not very efficient firm.

(a) A: Perhaps they didn't treat this order as urgent.
B: *Yes, it may/might not have been treated as urgent.*

A: Perhaps the Customs impounded the packet.
B: *Yes, it may/might have been impounded by the Customs.*

A third person reports these opinions later. The prompt is given to help the student to remember.

(b) *Prompt*: didn't treat this order as urgent.
C: *They thought that it might not have been treated as urgent.*

1–10 *Perhaps they . . .*

1 didn't deal with the order at once.
2 didn't post the packet promptly.
3 didn't mark it urgent.
4 didn't address it correctly.
5 didn't label it clearly.
6 didn't tie it up properly.
7 didn't send it by air.
8 didn't stamp it sufficiently.
9 didn't register it.
10 didn't insure it.

11–20 *Perhaps . . .*

11 the clerk overlooked the order.
12 the postman put it in the wrong box.
13 the postman delivered it to the wrong floor.
14 the postman left it next door.
15 the postman brought it to our old office.
16 the Customs delayed it. (*Keep* **the Customs.**)
17 the Customs returned it to the senders. (*Keep* **the Customs.**)
18 the Customs confiscated it. (*Keep* **the Customs.**)
19 the postal strike held it up.
20 a magpie stole it.

(b) As for (a), but in 1–10 omit *Perhaps they* and in 11–20 omit *Perhaps*.

88 Passive: **must** + phrasal verbs

☑ PEG 305B

A: About this parcel—do we have to tie it up?
B: *Oh, yes, it must be tied up.*

About . . . —do we have to . . .

1 these books . . . take them back?
2 these old newspapers . . . throw them away?
3 this broken glass . . . sweep it up?
4 this wallet we've found . . . hand it in?
5 these old curtains . . . take them down?
6 the carpet . . . roll it up?
7 this watch we are giving him . . . wrap it up?
8 this information . . . pass it on?
9 this notice . . . put it up?
10 the instructions . . . write them down?
11 these forms . . . fill them up?
12 the cases on the roofrack . . . strap them on?
13 the money . . . pay it back?
14 the dishes . . . wash them up?
15 his orders . . . carry them out?
16 the wall that you say is unsafe . . . pull it down?
17 the caravan . . . tow it away?
18 the documents . . . lock them up?
19 the meeting . . . put it off?
20 the weeds . . . pull them up?

89 Passive: **should** + present and perfect infinitives

☑ PEG 302D

It is Thursday evening. The secretary is inclined to leave everything till Friday, which doesn't please the boss. But perhaps the secretary has too many duties.

A: I'll remove the old newspapers tomorrow.

(a) B: *But they should be removed every day.* (stress on **every**)
(b) B: *But they should have been removed today.* (stress on **today**)

I'll . . . tomorrow.

1 open your windows
2 dust your desk
3 tidy your books
4 water your pot plants
5 wind your clock
6 empty your wastepaper basket
7 wash your coffee cup
8 clean your office
9 clear your out-tray
10 refill your cigar-box
11 enter the expenses
12 check the petty cash
13 test the alarm system
14 pay in the cheques (*Keep* **in.**)
15 lock the grille
16 change the combination of the safe
17 report the absentees
18 write up the diary (*Keep* **up.**)
19 file the copies
20 exercise the guard dogs

90 Passive: **used to** + infinitive

☐ PEG 302D

A: They serve wine once a week.
B: *It used to be served twice a week, didn't it?* (stress on **twice**)

A: The hospital allows visitors once a day.
B: *They used to be allowed twice a day, didn't they?*

1 They make tea once a day.
2 They sweep the street once a week.
3 The office issues season tickets once a month.
4 They deliver mail once a day.
5 They lower the safety curtain once in every performance.
6 The doctor weighs the children once a term.
7 They test our company car once a year.
8 They publish the paper once a month.
9 The announcer gives weather reports once a day.
10 Someone inspects restaurants every year.
11 We test the students once a term.
12 We admit new students once a term.
13 We elect new officers once a year.
14 They read the news (on the radio) once a day.
15 They play the national anthem once a day.
16 They empty the dustbin once a week.
17 Someone washes my windows once a month.
18 They drain the swimming pool once a year.
19 They change the film once a week.
20 They service the lift once a year.

91 Passive: **will have/would have** + infinitive

☑ PEG 302D

(a) Bill has bought a house and he and a friend are discussing repairs and
alterations. The friend speaks first:

A: You'll repair the gate, I suppose?
B: *Oh, yes, the gate will have to be repaired.*

(b) Bill is looking over a house which is for sale. He and his friend are
considering what repairs would be necessary if he bought it.

A: You'd repair the gate, I suppose?
B: *Oh, yes, the gate would have to be repaired.*

(a) *You'll . . . I suppose?*

1 replace the broken panes,
2 retile the roof,
3 repair the gutters,
4 sweep the chimneys,
5 redecorate the hall,
6 paint the woodwork,
7 repaper the sitting room,
8 install central heating,
9 move the kitchen,
10 rewire the basement,
11 change the locks,
12 strengthen the balconies,
13 put in a skylight,
14 see to the drains,
15 mend the fence,
16 clip the hedge,
17 cut back the bushes,
18 prune the apple trees,
19 fill up the holes in the path,
20 rebuild the garage,

(b) *You'd . . . I suppose?*

1 replace the broken panes,
2 retile the roof,
etc.

92 Reported speech: statements reported by **he says** or **he said**

☐ PEG 308A,B

Alan is coming to spend a few days with the Smiths. He phones from the station. Betty Smith answers.

(a) She reports Alan's remarks to her husband while the conversation is still going on.

A: I'm phoning from the station.
B: *He says he's phoning from the station.*

(b) This time, Betty reports the conversation later.

B: *He said he was phoning from the station.*

1 I've just arrived.
2 We were delayed two hours by a blocked line.
3 The station is packed with football fans from my home town.
4 I can hardly hear you; they are making such a noise.
5 I'll try to get a taxi.
6 But this may take some time as all the football fans seem to want taxis too. (*Use* **it** *for* **this**.)
7 I may have to leave my luggage in the station and get a bus.
8 I hope to be with you in about an hour. (*Use* **us**.)
9 I have a French girl with me called Marie Celeste.
10 Her brother asked me to look after her.
11 We're waiting for her friends but I don't see any sign of them.
12 If they don't turn up I'll have to bring Marie with me.
13 I hope you won't mind.
14 I'm sure you'll like her.
15 She is the most charming girl I have ever met.
16 I'm going to try to get her a job in my college.
17 It's very good of you to put me up. (*Use* **us**.)
18 I'm afraid I can only stay three days.
19 I'm looking forward to seeing you again very much. (*Use* **us**.)
20 I've got lots of messages for you from my family. (*Use* **us**.)

93 Reported speech: **suggest** + gerund

☑ PEG 289D

A students' club are planning a holiday abroad. The committee is now discussing where to go and what to do. Three members make suggestions.

(a) The chairman repeats each suggestion to make sure that the rest of the committee have heard it:

A (=PAUL): Shall we start on Friday?
B: *Paul suggests starting on Friday.*

A (=BILL): Hotels are too dear. Let's camp out.
B: *Bill says hotels are too dear and suggests camping out.*

(b) The secretary reports the suggestions afterwards to someone who wasn't at the meeting:

A (=BILL): Friday's too soon. Let's wait till Saturday.
B: *Bill said that Friday was too soon and suggested waiting till Saturday.*

See also Drills 28 and 29.

1 Shall we hitch-hike? (**Paul**)
2 There are too many of us. Let's go on motor cycles. (**Bill**)
3 That's too uncomfortable. Why don't we hire cars? (**Ann**)
4 It would cost too much. What about borrowing the college bus? (**Bill**)
5 Shall we sleep in Youth Hostels? (**Bill**)
6 Let's camp out. (**Paul**)
7 Why not rent a caravan? (**Ann**)
8 Shall we pick fruit and make some money? (**Paul**)
9 Fruit picking is hard work. Let's spend the day on the beach. (**Bill**)
10 (And) let's visit museums and art galleries. (**Ann**)
11 Shall we eat in restaurants? (**Ann**)
12 Let's have meals in the caravan. (**Paul**)
13 Why don't we cook over an open fire? (**Bill**)
14 Let's pack plenty of tinned food and Coca Cola. (**Paul**)
15 Let's buy food locally. (**Ann**)
16 Why not drink the local wine? (**Bill**)
17 Shall we find out about pop festivals? (**Bill**)
18 Let's look out for classical concerts. (**Ann**)
19 Why don't we bring guitars and make our own music? (**Paul**)
20 Why don't we split into three groups? (**Bill**)

94 Reported speech: questions

☐ PEG 317

Alan is thinking of buying a car. He asks a colleague, Bill, a number of questions, which Bill later reports to another car-owner.

A: Have you (got) a car?
B: *He asked if I had a car.*
or
He asked me if I had a car.

A: Do you have it serviced regularly?
B: *He asked if I had it serviced regularly.*

1 What kind of car have you (got)? (**got** *can be omitted.*)
2 What does it cost you to run it?
3 How many kilometres does it do the litre?
4 Does it belong to you or you and your wife?
5 Can your wife drive?
6 Is she a safe driver?
7 How many kilometres do you drive in a month?
8 Did you pass your test the first time?
9 Do you think driving tests are any use?
10 Do you give lifts?
11 How long have you been driving?
12 Have you ever had an accident?
13 Was it your own fault?
14 Do you do your own repairs?
15 What would you do if petrol doubled in price?
16 Do you always wear a safety belt?
17 Do you take the car to work?
18 Are you thinking of getting a new car?
19 Do you let your wife take the car shopping?
20 Don't you think it unwise to let your wife drive?

95 Reported speech: questions

☑ PEG 317

Mrs Adams, who is rather inquisitive, wants to know about Mrs
Brown's new tenant. Mrs Brown reports the questions to her husband.

A: Who is he?
B: *She asked me who he was.* (**me** is not essential.)

A: What does he do for a living?
B: *She asked me what he did for a living.* (**me** is not essential.)

1 How long has he been here?
2 Where does he come from?
3 Does he teach in the Technical College?
4 How long has he been working there?
5 Is he married?
6 Where is his wife?
7 Does he get many letters?
8 Where do his letters come from?
9 Where does he do his shopping?
10 Does he do his own cooking?
11 Do you clean his flat?
12 Has he a car?
13 Does he ever speak to you?
14 What does he do in the evenings?
15 Does he go away at the weekends?
16 Does he wear a wig?
17 Why has he shaved off his beard?
18 Is he thinking of buying a house here?
19 Why is Mrs Jones suspicious of him?
20 What do your other tenants think of him?

96 Reported speech: **want** + object + infinitive

■ PEG 243A

Mr Jones calls Ann into his office and gives her some instructions. She then returns to the main office and tells a colleague what she has been asked to do.

    A: Would you please file these letters?

(a) B: *He wants me to file some letters.* (She hasn't filed them yet.)

(b) B: *He wanted me to file some letters.* (**wanted** implies that she has already filed them or that she couldn't or wouldn't file them.)

(c) B: *He asked/told me to file them.* (This merely reports the request.)

Use **a** for **this**, **some** for **these** and **his** for **my**.

Would you please . . .

1 copy this contract?
2 correct this spelling mistake?
3 add something to this letter?
4 pin up these notices in the canteen?
5 look up our MP's address?
6 order some more paperclips?
7 contact our American branch?
8 send this report to our head office?
9 check these figures?
10 bring your tape recorder to the meeting?
11 type out a full report?
12 put these documents in my dispatch case?
13 lock my dispatch case?
14 leave the key on my desk?
15 take these books back to the library?
16 buy some flowers for my wife?
17 tell my wife I won't be home tonight?
18 remind the cleaners to empty my ashtray?
19 advertise for a new office boy?
20 book two plane tickets for New York?

97 Reported speech: **advise/warn** + object + infinitive

☐ PEG 320A, D

Bill is at his office, where he has just heard that he has won £100,000.
Ann, his secretary, and Tom, a colleague, are giving him advice, which
he later reports to a friend he meets on the train home.

A (=ANN): Why don't you give up your job?
B: *Ann advised me to give up my job.*

A (=TOM): Don't do anything in a hurry.
B: *Tom warned me not to do anything in a hurry.*

Tom's advice consists entirely of warnings, so it is best reported by
warned, though **advised** would also be possible.)

1 I should send out for a bottle of champagne. (**Ann**)
2 You'd better wait till lunchtime. (**Tom**)
3 Why don't you spend £1,000 on a terrific holiday? (**Ann**)
4 Don't change your way of living too quickly. (**Tom**)
5 Invite all your neighbours to a party. (**Ann**)
6 Don't begin entertaining too lavishly. (**Tom**)
7 You'd better give some of it to a charity. (**Ann**)
8 Don't offer to help everyone. (**Tom**)
9 I should get a new car. (**Ann**)
10 Don't go on a spending spree. (**Tom**)
11 Why don't you ring your wife and pass on the good news? (**Ann**)
12 You'd better not talk about it too much. (**Tom**)
13 Ask your wife what she'd like as a present. (**Ann**)
14 Don't give her a blank cheque. (**Tom**)
15 Why don't you tell her to go out and buy some new clothes? (**Ann**)
16 Don't encourage her to be extravagant. (**Tom**)
17 Why don't you visit your sister in Australia? (**Ann**)
18 You'd better see your tax inspector first. (**Tom**)
19 I should buy presents for all the children. (**Ann**)
20 Don't give them the impression that you are going to keep them in
   idleness for the rest of their lives. (**Tom**)

98 Reported speech: requests reported by **ask/want** + object + infinitive

☑ PEG 284, 320

Mr and Mrs Butt are booking in at a hotel. Mr Butt talks to the receptionist. Mrs Butt, who is a little deaf, doesn't hear the conversation clearly and asks her husband afterwards, who reports the receptionist's requests.

(a) A (=receptionist): If you'd leave your passport . . .

B: *She asked me to leave my passport.*

A: Please don't leave the lift doors open.

B: *She asked me not to leave the lift doors open.* (**warned** would also be possible.)

Alternatively Mrs Butt may want each sentence reported at once:

(b) A: If you'd leave your passport . . .

B: *She wants me to leave my passport.* (**asks** is possible but would be less usual.)

A: Please don't leave the lift doors open.

B: *She is asking/is warning me not to leave the lift doors open.* (**doesn't want me** to is possible but less emphatic.)

1 Could you show me your passport please?
2 If you'd fill up this form . . . (*Use* **the** for **this**.)
3 Would you sign the register, please?
4 Please write down the number of your car. (*Use* **our**.)
5 Please don't leave anything valuable in the car.
6 Please don't park outside the hotel.
7 Would you put your car in the hotel garage?
8 If you'd give the keys to the hall porter . . .
9 Please don't smoke in the garage.
10 Would you please read the Fire Instructions?

From now on, use *She asked/wants/is asking/is warning* **us**.

11 If you'd shut the lift gates after you . . .
12 Please don't allow your children to play with the lift.
13 Please tell me if you'd like an early call.
14 Could you let me know if you are going to be in for dinner?
15 Don't bring your dog into the dining room, please.
16 Would you hang your keys on this board when you are going out? (*Use* **the**.)
17 Could you vacate your room by noon on the day you are leaving?
18 Ring for room service if you want anything.
19 Would you inform the hall porter if you're going to be out late?
20 Please don't make too much noise after midnight.

99 Reported speech: commands reported by **tell/warn/want**
+ object + infinitive, or **say** + subject + **be** + infinitive

◪ PEG 320, 321

A supervisor is giving instructions to a group of exam candidates. One of these, Bill, reports the instructions after the exam.

(a) A: Sit at the numbered desks.
B: *He told us to sit at the numbered desks.*

A: Don't smoke.
B: *He told/warned us not to smoke.*

Bill also reports the instructions immediately they are given to another candidate who doesn't hear very well.

(b) A: Sit at the numbered desks.
B: *He says we're to sit at the numbered desks.*
or
B: *He wants us to sit at the numbered desks.*

A: Don't smoke.
B: *He says we're not to smoke.*
or
B: *He warns us not to smoke.*

warn could also be used to report an affirmative command—A: Watch the time. B: *He warned us to watch the time.*

1 Hang up your coats.
2 Don't write in the margin.
3 Put your name on each sheet.
4 Read the questions carefully.
5 Start each question on a fresh sheet.
6 Answer the questions in order.
7 Don't spend too long on the first question.
8 Don't talk to your neighbour.
9 Don't try to copy your neighbour's answers.
10 Keep to the point.
11 Watch the time.
12 Be careful about your spelling.
13 Write clearly.
14 Count the number of words in your essays.
15 Look over your work before you hand it in.
16 Number your sheets.
17 Tie the sheets together.
18 Go out quietly when you've finished.
19 Don't take any paper out of the room.
20 Come back at two o'clock.

100 Reported speech: commands reported by **say** + subject + **be** + infinitive

☑ PEG 321

Mr Jones, a widower, has to go away for a fortnight, leaving his house and two children in the care of his neighbour, Ann. He gives Ann various instructions, which she reports to her husband.

    A: If one of the children gets ill, ring the doctor.

(a) B: *He says that if one of the children gets ill I am to ring the doctor.*

(b) B: *He said that if one of the children got ill I was to call a doctor.*

Up to the time that Mr Jones goes away Ann could use either form. After he has left she would be more likely to use the second.

1 If one of the children loses his appetite take his temperature.
2 If the temperature is very high ring the doctor.
3 If one of them cuts himself wash the cut and put on a plaster.
4 When they have finished their homework let them watch TV.
5 When they are in bed read them a story.
6 If it gets cold make them wear coats.
7 If they miss the school bus send them by taxi.
8 When you go out double-lock the door.
9 If the cat is still out when you go to bed leave a window open.
10 If you haven't time to cook open tins.
11 When you've used up the tins on the shelf buy some more.
12 If you run out of oil order another supply.
13 If it gets colder turn on the central heating.
14 If the central heating doesn't work properly phone the company.
15 If the dogs won't eat tinned food buy them fresh meat.
16 If the dogs bark at night go down and see what it is.
17 If the tank leaks send for the plumber.
18 If any letters come for me please forward them.
19 If the gardener turns up ask him to cut the grass.
20 When the milkman brings his bill please pay it.

Key

For each drill the first answer is always given in full as a pattern, e.g.
Yes, but I like **doing** housework.

In the pattern answers:

The words in *italic* type form part of all the other answers.

The words in ordinary type are a repetition of part of the original
sentence.

The words in **bold** type are the work of the student, who normally has
to change the form of the original verb.

The rest of the answers are given, wholly or in part, only where they
may be found difficult. They are printed in ordinary type. Where the
change to be made by the student is very simple, e.g. from infinitive to
gerund, separate answers for each question are not given.

Drill 1 (a) *Yes, but I like* **doing** housework. (b) *Yes, but I liked* **doing**
housework. (c) *Yes, but I don't/didn't mind* **doing** housework.
(d) *Yes, but I enjoy/enjoyed* **doing** housework.

In nos. 14, 15 and 16 use **my** instead of 'your'.

Drill 2 Questions: (a) *You like* **sweeping** streets, *don't you?*
(b) *You liked* **sweeping** streets, *didn't you?*

Answers: *Yes, but I wouldn't like/wouldn't care/would hate* **to sweep**
streets *for a living.*

Drill 3 (a) *So have I. I like* **hoovering** carpets *but hate* **dusting**
furniture. (b) *So have I. I enjoy* **hoovering** carpets *but don't care for*
dusting furniture. (c) *So have I. I don't mind* **hoovering** carpets but
dislike **dusting** furniture.

Drill 4 (a) *My brother prefers* **singing** in a choir *to* **singing** solo *too.*
(slight stress on **my**) (b) *My brother likes* **singing** in a choir *better than*
singing solo *too.*

Drill 5 Questions: *What about* **writing**? *Or would you rather* **phone**?
Answers: (a) *I'd rather* **write** (*than* **phone**). (b) *I'd prefer* **to**
write. (c) *I'm against* **phoning**. (d) *I'm for* **phoning**. (e) *I'm in*
favour of **phoning**.

Key

Drill 6 (a) *I'd prefer you* **to phone him** today (infinitive with 'to').

(b) *I'd rather you* **phoned him** *today.* 2. brought them 3. spoke to him 4. swept them 5. began 6. paid it 7. came 8. left 9. went there/went to it 10. read them 11. lent it to him 12. took them back 13. gave it to her 14. burnt it 15. sent it to him 16. got it 17. wrote to them 18. saw to it 19. bought it 20. made them

Drill 7 (a) *No, I'd like you* to lead the deputation. (stress on *you*)
(b) *No, I want you* to lead the deputation. (stress on *you*)

Drill 8 (a) *No, I would like to have* **rung him** *but there wasn't time.*
2. talked to them 3. attended it 4. tried it 5. watched it
6. visited it 7. seen it 8. walked round it 9. met them 10. looked at it 11. climbed to the top of it 12. had some 13. painted some
14. made one 15. taken some 16. hired one 17. strolled round it 18. sent some 19. bought some 20. listened to it.

(b) *No, I wanted* **to ring him** *but there wasn't time.* Answers for (b) as for (a) but with *wanted* + infinitive.

Drill 9 (a) and (b) *Yes, but apparently her husband doesn't want her* **to paint.** (stress on *want*)

(b) *Yes, but apparently her husband didn't want her* **to paint.**

Drill 10 *Oh, just go to the office and say that you wish* **to enrol** for a course.

Drill 11 (a) *Yes, I wish he'd* **pay** him *more regularly.* Answers for (a) as for (b) below but with *I wish he'd* + infinitive.

(b) *Yes, I wish he* **paid him** *more regularly.* 2. cleaned it 3. tidied up 4. defrosted it 5. changed them 6. swept it 7. washed them 8. cut it 9. shaved 10. did it 11. put them out
12. cooked for himself 13. opened them 14. emptied them
15. attended them 16. wrote them 17. answered them 18. had them cleaned 19. took them back 20. watered them

Drill 12 *I don't know. I wish I* **hadn't gone** into the pub. Or, as for 3: *I don't know. I wish I* **had made** him eat something.

Drill 13 (a) *Yes, he admitted* **forging it.** (b) *No, he denied* **forging it.** (c) *No, but he is suspected of* **forging it.** (d) *No, but he has been accused of/charged with* **forging it.**

102

2. planning it   3. taking part in it   4. hijacking it   5. kidnapping
her   6. firing at him   7. attacking her   8. shooting him
9. threatening him   10. sending them   11. receiving them
12. selling it   13. giving false evidence   14. intimidating them
15. bribing them   16. starting them   17. derailing it   18. leading
it   19. drugging them   20. helping them to escape

Drill 14   *Then try to avoid* **getting** *very angry.*   7. making long
speeches   9. carrying heavy suitcases   15. sleeping in haunted rooms

Drill 15   *Do you actually enjoy* **peeling** *potatoes?*   8. polishing
silver   18. rearranging furniture

Drill 16   *Fancy/Imagine* **not enjoying** *one's/her days off!* (This is the
pattern for comments on negative statements.)   3. *Fancy/Imagine*
refusing *a rise in salary!* (This is the pattern for comments on
affirmative statements.)

Drill 17   *Oh, I'll have you* **skating** *by the end of the month.*

Drill 18   *I couldn't help* **coughing**.   13. disturbing you all
19. treading on your toe

Drill 19   *But she keeps* **coming** *late.*   15. ringing up her friends
19. switching on her radio   20. spelling my name wrong

Drill 20   (a) *Well, I won't come if it means* **getting up** *at five.*   (b) *But
I'm not used to* **getting up** *at five.*   (c) *Yes, you'll soon get used to*
getting up *at five.*

Drill 21   *Yes. Would you mind* **making them**?   5. working it out
9. putting it on

Drill 22   (a) *Oh, I don't mind him/his* **borrowing** *from the petty
cash.*   (b) *I object to him/his* **borrowing** *from the petty cash.*
(c) *I won't have him* **borrowing** *from the petty cash.*
4. getting my secretary   18. smoking my cigars   20. chasing my
secretary

Drill 23   Pattern for 1–10: *It's very difficult to prevent people* **having**
picnics.
Pattern for 11–20: *It's very difficult to prevent children* **shouting and
screaming**.   12. carving their names on trees   13. writing things on
walls

Drill 24   (a) *I don't remember* **arriving** drunk.

(b) *Oh, yes, you did. I saw you* **bringing** *two drunk friends.*
3. heard   4. heard   5. heard   6. heard   7. saw   8. saw
9. saw   10. saw   11. saw   12. heard   13. heard   14. heard you
waking the people/heard the people in the next flat complaining
15. heard   16. saw/heard   17. saw   18. saw   19. heard   20. saw

Drill 25   *I don't remember* **her being** rude.   2. them/their singing
3. them/their forgetting   4. them/their refusing   5. it/its breaking
6. them/their going   7. you/your losing   8. them/their getting   9. it/
its creaking   10. them/their rattling   11. it/its being   12. them/their
running   13. them/their whistling   14. them/their cheating   15. it/its
raining   16. him/his insulting   17. you/your suffering   18. them/their
overcharging   19. them/their mixing   20. you/your being

Drill 26   (a) *You should tell him to stop* **arguing.**   (b) *Why don't you tell
him to stop* **arguing?**   (c) *Can't you get him to stop* **arguing?**   (d) *Can't
you stop him* **arguing?**

Drill 27   *But how could you stop him* **leaving home?** (stress on *you* or
stop)

Drill 28   *Actually, Ann suggested* **recording** *his conversation but I
didn't think it was necessary.*

Drill 29   *Well, I suggested* **leaving** *at once but Tom wouldn't hear of it.*

Drill 30   (a) *I never suggested* **them/their wearing** masks. (stress on
I)   (b) *I never suggested that* **they (should) wear** masks.   (c) *I never
suggested that* **they wore** masks.   (d) *I never told/advised them* **to wear**
masks.

Drill 31   *Yes, let's try* **oiling** the hinges.

Drill 32   *Yes, they want/need* **painting.**   11. tying up   16. cutting
off   19. propping up   20. cleaning out

Drill 33   (a) *Yes, I suppose he was afraid of* **missing** his train.   (b) *Yes,
he probably didn't want to risk* **missing** his train.

Drill 34   *But I'm not interested in* **becoming** a celebrity.

Drill 35   (a) *Yes, I'm used to* **clocking** in and out.   (b) *Yes, but you'll
soon get used to* **clocking** in and out.   (c) *Oh, I'm getting used to*

clocking in and out.   (d) *Oh, I've got used to* **clocking** in and out.
(e) *Oh, I soon got used to* **clocking** in and out.   (f) *Oh, you soon get used to* **clocking** in and out.

Drill 36   (a) *I don't feel like* **walking** to the village.   (b) *He suggests/ suggested* **walking** to the village.

Drill 37   (a) *Well, I hope they punished him for* **kicking** a football through the greenhouse roof.   (b) *Well, I hope he apologized for* **kicking** a football through the greenhouse roof.   (c) *Poor Tom. I expect he got into trouble for* **kicking** a football through the greenhouse roof.

Drill 38   *No, I had a lot of difficulty* (*in*) **fitting** everything into my case.

Drill 39   (a) *Do you have any difficulty* (*in*) **regulating** the central heating?
(b) *No, I find it quite easy* **to regulate** it.
In all (b) answers, the first *it* is invariable. It is part of the structure. The final pronoun, however, will vary with the object. Final pronouns are as follows:
2. it   3. them   4. them   5. them   6. them   7. them   8. it
9. them   10. them   11. them   12. them   13. it   14. it   15. it
16. them   17. them   18. them   19. them   20. it
(c) *No, I find it quite easy* **to regulate**.
Note that here there is no final pronoun. But the first pronoun will change with the object. For example:
2. I find it easy to organize.   3. I find them easy to control.   4. I find them easy to remember.   5. I find them easy to answer.
Pronouns are as in the answers for (b).

Drill 40   (a) *It's no use* **talking** to him.   (b) *It's no use my* **talking** to him. (stress on *my*)   (c) *It's no use my* **talking** to him, *but if you talked to him something might be done.* (stress on *my* and *you*)

Drill 41   (a) *Yes, he insisted on* **wearing** a tie.   (b) *Yes, he insisted on my/me* **wearing** a tie.

Drill 42   *But in spite of* **knowing** no Spanish, he got the job.
2. starting last, he   3. drinking a lot, he   4. missing the first train, she   5. having no passports, they   6. practising a lot, he   7. dieting for six months, she   8. working hard, he   9. studying for ten years,

he   10. using very expensive cameras, he   11. paying a lot for her clothes, she   12. living quite near the office, she   13. doing no work, he   14. being widely advertised, it   15. spending his life in this country, he

Drill 43   *Yes, I'm looking forward to* **swimming** in the sea.

Drill 44   *Oh, she makes a point of* **arriving** in a Rolls Royce. *She wants to attract attention.*

Drill 45   (a) *But if the train doesn't leave till 9, there's no point in* **setting out** for the station at 7.
In (b), replace *There's no point in* by *What's the point of.*

Drill 46   (a) *Oh, he succeeded in* **passing it,** did he?   (b) *Oh, he managed* **to pass it,** did he?

Drill 47   (a) *I didn't hear* it **whistling.** (stress on *I*)   (b) *I heard it* **whistling,** *but it didn't keep me awake.*

Drill 48   *Yes, I hear* **him singing.**   2. him whistling   3. them quarrelling   4. it crying   5. them barking   6. her coughing   7. him walking about   8. them arguing   9. it going off   10. him swearing   11. her hoovering   12. her using   13. them tap-dancing   14. him practising   15. them complaining   16. her nagging   17. him hammering   18. them screaming   19. them running   20. them banging

Drill 49   (a) *Yes, I heard* **him booking them.**
2. him inviting her   3. her accepting it   4. her telling him   5. them shutting   6. him winding it   7. it ringing   8. them accusing him   9. it stopping   10. it cracking   11. him speaking to her   12. them shouting at him   13. him apologizing   14. her asking for them   15. him complaining about it   16. him explaining   17. her cancelling it   18. him threatening them   19. them laughing   20. them opening it
(b) *Yes, I heard* **him book them.**

Drill 50   *But you see people* **jumping the queue** *in our country too!*

Drill 51   (a) *Well, I didn't actually see him* **signing it.**   2. locking it   3. taking it   4. reading them   5. using it   6. weighing it   7. posting it   8. burning them   9. copying them   10. burying it   11. throwing it   12. attacking her   13. giving it   14. sterilizing it

15. swallowing it   16. oiling them   17. drinking it   18. cutting it
19. opening it   20. taking it

(b) *Well, I didn't actually see him* **sign it.**

Drill 52   (a) *Yes, I* **saw it stopping.**   2. them leaping out   3. them
dashing into the bank   4. him demanding them   5. them smashing
it   6. her screaming   7. them shouting at her   8. it going off
9. them arriving   10. them rushing out   11. them seizing her
12. them threatening to kill her   13. them dragging her towards their
car   14. him ordering them to release her   15. them firing at him
16. him ordering them to fire back   17. them running for cover
18. him falling   19. him lying bleeding on the ground   20. them
surrendering

(b) *Yes, I* **saw it stop.**

Drill 53   *Well, I saw a few of them* **climbing** over the wall. (stress on
few)   4. Well, I heard a few of them making a horrible noise. (stress on
few)

Drill 54   *Yes, I spent all yesterday afternoon* **tidying up.**

Drill 55   (a) *Oh, I'd better* **pay** my bills. (stress on *I* and *my*)   (b) *Oh, I
suppose it's time I* **paid** my bills. (stress on *I* and *my*)

Drill 56   (a) and (b) *But why didn't you let him* **stop?**   (c) *Why on earth
didn't you let him* **stop?**

Drill 57   (a) *Our parents wouldn't let us* **run about** without shoes.
(b) *We weren't allowed to* **run about** without shoes.

Drill 58   *But why do you let him* **kick** *his brother?* (stress on *let*)

Drill 59   (a) *Yes, I made him* **apologize.**   2. explain   3. pay it
4. write to them   5. clean it   6. take it   7. report it   8. wait for her
9. ring them   10. finish it   11. answer it   12. make it   13. clean
them   14. change them   15. wear it   16. move it   17. insure it
18. fasten it   19. did them   20. check them

(b) *Yes. I made him* **hang it up.**   2. turn it down   3. shave it off
4. take them back   5. pick them up   6. keep it on   7. take it
down   8. roll it up   9. lock them up   10. throw them away   11. fill it
up   12. look it up   13. switch it off   14. pay it back   15. put them
away

Key

Drill 60 (a) *You should have made them all* **drink** *milk.* (b) *The boys should have been made to* **drink** *milk too.*

Drill 61 *No, I just happened to* **be** *in the phone box.* 2. *No, I just happened to* **be looking at my** *watch.* (Use **my** for 'your' throughout.)

Drill 62 (a) *Well, I meant to* **swim** *before breakfast but the weather wasn't suitable.* (b) *Well, we were meant to* **swim** *before breakfast but the weather wasn't suitable.* (c) *Well, we were to have* **swum** *before breakfast but the weather wasn't suitable.*

Drill 63 *No, it never occurred to me* **to invite her.** 2. offer him a drink 3. write to her 4. thank them 5. make him some 6. put him up 7. ring him 8. say hello 9. congratulate her 10. apologize to him 11. keep her a place 12. tell them a story 13. wait for him 14. send him a present 15. help them with their luggage 16. show her the way 17. give him a lift 18. see her home 19. wish him luck 20. kiss her

Drill 64 *He offered to* **wait for** *me too but I refused.* (stress on 'me' and *too*) 7. *He offered to* **wash** *my car too/mine too, but I refused.* ('mine' can be used instead of 'my' + noun in nos. 7, 9, 13, 16, 17, 18, 19 and 20.)

Drill 65 (a) *Oh, Ann always forgets* **to turn them out.** (b) *Oh, Ann never remembers* **to turn them out.**
2. switch it off 3. shut them 4. pay him 5. take it in 6. wash them 7. make it 8. sweep it 9. dust them 10. put them up 11. water them 12. thank them 13. put it out 14. stamp them 15. check it 16. buy them 17. feed them 18. cover them 19. set it 20. lock it

Drill 66 *Well, he seems* **to be** *afraid of someone.*

Drill 67 *Well, he seems to be* **talking to her** *today.*
2. helping her 3. using it 4. trying to please her 5. wearing one 6. playing with them 7. bringing her some 8. taking some 9. doing it 10. carrying them 11. leaving it 12. letting her 13. quarrelling with them 14. shouting at them 15. walking 16. paying 17. collecting them 18. reading it 19. waiting for her 20. shaking it

Drill 68   (a) *Yes, he seems to have* **lived** here **most of his life.**   (b) *Yes, he appears to have* **lived** here **most of his life.**   (c) *Yes, he is said to have* **lived** here **most of his life.**   (d) *Yes, he is supposed to have* **lived** here **most of his life.**
2. married several times   3. had a lot of children   4. built several other houses   5. owned enormous estates   6. employed a huge staff   7. been an excellent landlord   8. liked him very much   9. entertained lavishly   10. drunk heavily   11. hunted when he was a young man   12. kept racehorses all his life   13. won quite a lot of races   14. lost a fortune gambling   15. sold two of them   16. quarrelled with some of them   17. fought two   18. killed his opponent both times   19. left the country after the second duel   20. died in Paris

Drill 69   *No, I used* **to smoke** *a lot but I don't now.*
18. argue with him   19. quarrel with her

Drill 70   *Is he? I used to* **wash up** *too, but I don't now.*
2. Has he? I used to shave   3. Does he? I used to go   4. Does he? I used to cut   5. Does he? I used to wash   6. Does he? I used to read   7. Did he? I used to take   8. Is he? I used to empty   9. Is he? I used to sew on   10. Has he? I used to polish   11. Does he? I used to wear   12. Does he? I used to sweep   13. Does he? I used to go   14. Did he? I used to get up   .15. Does he? I used to write   16. Does he? I used to give   17. Is he? I used to save   18. Has he? I used to make   19. Does he? I used to stamp   20. Does he? I used to clean

Drill 71   (a) *No, I was afraid to* **jump out.**   (b) *No, I didn't dare to* **jump out.**
2. climb down   3. use it   4. complain   5. drink it   6. interrupt him   7. contradict him   8. mention it to her   9. tell them   10. inform them   11. open it   12. go out at night   13. say anything   14. appeal   15. answer it

Drill 72   *I was* **horrified to hear** cries of pain coming from the next room.
2. astonished to see   3. annoyed to find   4. glad to see   5. delighted to receive   6. surprised to find   7. dismayed to hear   8. shocked to find   9. appalled to see   10. amazed to hear   11. relieved to find   12. disappointed to hear   13. annoyed to hear   14. appalled to

see   15. horrified to hear   16. relieved to hear   17. pleased to
find   18. glad to see   19. sorry to find   20. delighted to hear

Drill 73   *It was* good **of them to wait for me.**
2. kind of him to lend   3. stupid of her to believe   4. nice of them to
invite   5. sensible of her to tell   6. clever of you to find   7. careless
of her to leave   8. rash of him to have   9. prudent of him to ask
10. idiotic of her to argue   11. selfish of him to refuse   12. cowardly
of them to run away   13. dishonest of him to keep   14. greedy of him
to take   15. brave of her to jump   16. generous of him to offer
17. mean of him to suggest   18. unkind of him to say   19. wicked of
him to tell   20. courageous of him to admit

Drill 74   *What a* **funny place to live!**
2. an odd thing to study   3. a silly place to park   4. a slow way to
travel   5. a rude thing to say   6. an uncomfortable place to sleep
7. an interesting way to make   8. an odd time to swim   9. a strange
place to play   10. an extraordinary place to make decisions   11. an
odd thing to live on   12. a queer place to cook   13. an inconvenient
time to ring up   14. an unsafe place to keep money   15. a noisy place
to spend one's free time   16. an odd way to relax   17. a strange thing
to read   18. an unpleasant time to get up   19. an agreeable time to
have a holiday   20. an expensive car to drive

Drill 75   (a) *No, he was too* **young to go** alone.
2. too fat to get   3. too drunk to drive   4. too impatient to wait
5. too weak to walk   6. too ill to eat   7. too poor to buy   8. too
stupid to understand   9. too heavy to ride   10. too excited to
listen   11. too short to wear   12. too big to become   13. too
discouraged to apply   14. too unenterprising to try   15. too mean to
give us   16. too proud to admit   17. too conventional to wear
18. too cautious to lend   19. too narrow-minded to sympathize
20. too polite to say

(b) *Yes, he was* **old** *enough* **to go** alone. Infinitives as above.

Drill 76   (a) *No, it was too* **sour to eat.**
2. too tough to grill   3. too thick to push under the door   4. too faint
to read   5. too high to see clearly   6. too big to put in the boot
7. too heavy to tow behind the car   8. too long to put in my
suitcase   9. too deep to wade   10. too wide to jump   11. too unripe

to pick   12. too fragile to send by post   13. too sour to use   14. too
hot to drink   15. too shabby to wear

(b) *Yes, it was* **sweet** *enough* **to eat.** Infinitives as above.

Drill 77   (a) *No, it was too* **wet to sleep** in.
2. too narrow to camp on   3. too thin to walk on   4. too rough to slide
down   5. too soft to land on   6. too hot to take out   7. too dim to
read by   8. too thick to see through   9. too high to dive from
10. too untidy to hand in   11. too polluted to swim in   12. too
unsteady to stand on   13. too shallow to dive into   14. too dirty to sit
on   15. too heavy to pick up

(b) *Yes, it was* **dry** *enough* **to sleep** in. Infinitives as above.

Drill 78   *No. He went to* Zurich **to arrange** a loan.

Drill 79   *All right. I won't* talk about traffic accidents *so as not to*
frighten *Mrs Jones.*
2. criticize . . . offend   3. play . . . disturb   4. tell . . . shock
5. make . . . wake   6. chew . . . disgust   7. bang . . . startle
8. say . . . depress   9. whistle . . . irritate   10. discuss . . .
worry   11. sing . . . annoy   12. smoke . . . upset   13. come . . .
bother   14. leave . . . inconvenience   15. mention . . . distress

Drill 80   (a) *I see. He* took the keys to the office *so that you couldn't/so
that you wouldn't be able to* **drive** the car.   (b) *I see. He* took the keys
to the office *to prevent you* **driving** the car.
The last part of the original sentence becomes the first part of the
answer.

Drill 81   *It was no accident.* He **left** his clothes on the beach *so that we
would* **think** he was drowned.   2. She placed the letter   3. She burnt
the document   4. He was wearing dark   5. He was sitting on the
letter   6. She gave us   7. She mentioned Tom's   8. He was standing
outside   9. They were speaking French   10. They left a bicycle
11. She left her umbrella   12. He posted all   13. He was in the
telephone box   14. She dropped the report   15. She dropped her
handkerchief

Drill 82   (a) *I'm not to let him* **climb** trees *in case* he **tears** his
trousers.   2. play . . . he falls   3. talk . . . he learns   4. run . . . he
tramples   5. strike . . . he burns   6. use . . . he cuts   7. stand . . .

he makes 8. pat . . . they bite 9. stroke . . . they scratch
10. shout . . . he disturbs 11. kick . . . he damages 12. sit . . . he
catches 13. cross . . . he is run over 14. go . . . he loses
15. carry . . . he drops 16. fly . . . he loses 17. sail . . . he
gets 18. throw . . . he breaks 19. help . . . he spills 20. ride . . .
he has

(b) *I wasn't allowed to let him* **climb** trees *in case* he **tore** his trousers.
Infinitives as in (a). 2. he fell 3. he learnt 4. he trampled 5. he
burnt 6. he cut 7. he made 8. they bit 9. they scratched 10. he
disturbed 11. he damaged 12. he caught 13. he was run
over 14. he lost 15. he dropped 16. he lost 17. he got 18. he
broke 19. he split/spilled 20. he had

(c) *She told me not to let him* **climb** trees *in case* he **tore** his trousers.

For remaining answers see (b).

Drill 83 *But you shouldn't have let him* **climb** trees. *He might have*
torn his trousers. Infinitives as in Drill 82. Past participles:
2. torn 3. fallen 4. learnt 5. burnt 6. cut 7. made
8. bitten 9. scratched 10. disturbed 11. damaged
12. caught 13. been run over 14. lost 15. dropped 16. lost
17. got 18. broken 19. spilt/spilled 20. had

Drill 84 (a) *Our* equipment **is serviced** *by students.* 2. are cleaned
3. is kept tidy 4. are cooked 5. are rung 6. are emptied
7. is manned 8. are replaced 9. is driven 10. is looked after
11. is organized 12. is produced 13. is run 14. are arranged
15. are collected 16. is drawn up 17. is printed 18. are done
19. is chosen 20. are appointed

(b) *Our* equipment **was serviced** *by students.* (c) *Our* equipment **has**
always been **serviced** *by students.* (d) *Our* equipment **should be**
serviced *by students.*

Drill 85 (a) *Oh, our* bridge **is** *being* **repainted** *too!* (b) *He said it was*
being **repainted.**

Verbs for (a) are given below. Verbs for (b) are the same, but with
was/were instead of **is/are**. 2. is . . . repaired 3. are . . .
widened 4. are . . . changed 5. is . . . rebuilt 6. are . . . taken
down 7. is . . . reopened 8. are . . . cleaned 9. is . . . closed
down 10. is . . . moved 11. are . . . replaced 12. is . . .

extended   13. are . . . rerouted   14. is . . . turned   15. is . . .
made   16. is . . . resurfaced   17. is . . . restored   18. is . . .
dredged   19. is . . . demolished   20. are . . . put up

Drill 86   (a) **It's** (= **it has**) *just been* **made**, *actually.*   (b) *No, when I
arrived,* **it** *had just been* **made.**

2. it . . . laid   3. they . . . opened   4. it . . . ground   5. they . . .
fried   6. they . . . washed   7. it . . . whipped   8. it . . . grated
9. it . . . sliced   10. they . . . boiled   11. they . . . shelled
12. it . . . carved   13. they . . . skinned   14. it . . . mixed
15. they . . . mashed   16. they . . . cored   17. they . . .
peeled   18. they . . . squeezed   19. it . . . grilled   20. they . . .
roasted

Drill 87   (a) 1–10 *Yes, it may/might not have been* **dealt with** at once.
11–20 *Yes, it may/might have been* overlooked.   (b) 1–10 *They thought
that it might not have been* **dealt with** at once. 11–20 *They thought that it
might have been* overlooked.

Drill 88   *Oh, yes,* **they** *must be* **taken back.**   2. they . . . thrown
away   3. it . . . swept up   4. it . . . handed in   5. they . . . taken
down   6. it . . . rolled up   7. it . . . wrapped up   8. it . . . passed
on   9. it . . . put up   10. they . . . written down   11. they . . . filled
up   12. they . . . strapped on   13. it . . . paid back   14. they . . .
washed up   15. they . . . carried out   16. it . . . pulled down
17. it . . . towed away   18. they . . . locked up   19. it . . . put
off   20. they . . . pulled up

Drill 89   (a) *But* **they** *should be* **opened** *every day.*   (b) *But* **they** *should
have been* **opened** *today.*

2. it . . . dusted   3. they . . . tidied   4. they . . . watered   5. it . . .
wound   6. it . . . emptied   7. it . . . washed   8. it . . . cleaned
9. it . . . cleared   10. it . . . refilled   11. they . . . entered
12. it . . . checked   13. it . . . tested   14. they . . . paid in
15. it . . . locked   16. it . . . changed   17. they . . . reported
18. it . . . written up   19. they . . . filed   20. they . . . exercised

Drill 90   **It** *used to be* **made** *twice* **a day,** *didn't it?* (stress on *twice*)
2. it . . . swept   3. they . . . issued   4. it . . . delivered   5. it . . .
lowered   6. they . . . weighed   7. it . . . tested   8. it . . .
published   9. they . . . given   10. they . . . inspected   11. they . . .

113

examined   12. they . . . admitted   13. they . . . elected   14. it . . .
read   15. it . . . played   16. it . . . emptied   17. they . . .
washed   18. it . . . drained   19. it . . . changed   20. it . . . serviced

Drill 91   (a) *Oh, yes*, the broken panes *will have to be* **replaced**.
(b) *Oh, yes*, the broken panes *would have to be* **replaced**.

Drill 92   (a) *He says* **he has** just arrived.   (b) *He said* **he had** just
arrived.

Answers for (a) require no change of tense, so only (b) answers are
given: 2. they had been delayed   3. was packed . . . from his   4. he
could hardly hear me . . . they were making   5. he'd try   6. it might
take   7. he might have to leave his   8. he hoped to be with us   9. he
had . . . with him   10. had asked him   11. they were . . . but he
didn't   12. if they didn't . . . he'd have to . . . with him   13. he hoped
I/we wouldn't mind   14. he was sure we'd like   15. she was . . . he
had   16. he was . . . at his   17. it was . . . of us to put him up
18. he was afraid he could   19. he was . . . to seeing us   20. he had
(got) . . . for us . . . from his

Drill 93   (a) *Paul suggests* **hitch-hiking**.

(b) 1. Paul suggested hitch-hiking.   2. Bill said that there were too
many of them and suggesting going   3. Ann said that was . . . and
suggested hiring   4. Bill said it would cost . . . and suggested
borrowing   5. Bill suggested sleeping   6. Paul suggested
camping   7. Ann suggested renting   8. Paul suggested picking . . .
and making   9. Bill said that fruit-picking was . . . and suggested
spending   10. Ann suggested visiting   11. Ann suggested eating
12. Paul suggested having   13. Bill suggested cooking   14. Paul
suggested packing   15. Ann suggested buying   16. Bill suggested
finding out   18. Ann suggested looking out   19. Paul suggested
bringing . . . and making their own   20. Bill suggested splitting

Drill 94   *He asked (me)* **what kind of car I had**.   2. what it cost me
3. how many kilometres it did   4. if it belonged to me or my wife   5. if
my wife could   6. if she was   7. how many kilometres I drove   8. if I
had passed my test   9. if I thought . . . were   10. if I gave   11. how
long I had been   12. if I had ever had   13. if it had been   14. if I
did   15. what I would do if   16. if I always wore   17. if I took   18. if
I was thinking   19. if I let my   20. if I didn't . . . to let my wife drive

Drill 95 *She asked (me)* **how long he had been here**.   2. where he came from   3. if he taught   4. how long he had been   5. if he was   6. where his wife was   7. if he got   8. where his letters came   9. where he did   10. if he did   11. if he cleaned   12. if he had   13. if he ever spoke to me   14. what he did   15. if he went   16. if he wore   17. why he had shaved   18. if he was thinking   19. why Mrs Jones was suspicious   20. what my other tenants thought

Drill 96   (a) *He wants me to* copy **a** contract.   (b) *He wanted me to* copy **a** contract.   (c) *He asked/told me to* copy **a** contract.

2. correct a   3. add something to a   4. pin up some   5. look up our   6. order some   7. contact our   8. send a   9. check some   10. bring my   11. type out a   12. put some documents in his   13. lock his   14. leave the key on his   15. take some/these   16. buy some flowers for his   17. tell his wife that he   18. remind the cleaners to empty his   19. advertise for a   20. book two

Drill 97   **Ann advised me to send out** for a bottle of champagne.
2. Tom warned me to wait till lunchtime   3. Ann advised me to spend   4. Tom warned me not to change my   5. Ann advised me to invite   6. Tom warned me not to begin   7. Ann advised me to give   8. Tom warned me not to offer   9. Ann advised me to get   10. Tom warned me not to go   11. Ann advised me to ring my   12. Tom warned me not to talk   13. Ann advised me to ask my   14. Tom warned me not to give   15. Ann advised me to tell   16. Tom warned me not to encourage   17. Ann advised me to visit my   18. Tom warned me to see my   19. Ann advised me to buy   20. Tom warned me not to give them

Nos. 3, 11, 15 and 17 could also be reported by 'Ann suggested' + gerund.

Drill 98   (a) *She* **asked me to show her my** passport.   2. asked me to fill up the form   3. asked me to sign the register   4. asked me to write down the number of our car   5. asked/warned me not to leave   6. asked me not to park   7. asked me to put my/our car   8. asked me to give the keys   9. asked/warned me not to smoke   10. asked/warned me to read   11. asked us to shut the gates after us   12. asked/warned us not to allow the children   13. asked us to tell her if we'd like   14. asked us to let her know if we were going   15. asked/warned us not to bring our   16. asked us to hang our keys

Key

on the board when we were going   17. asked us to vacate our room by
noon on the day we were   18. asked us to ring if we wanted
19. asked us to inform . . . if we were going   20. asked/warned us not
to make

(b) as for (a), but with 'wants'/'is asking'/'is warning' and with present
and continuous tenses left unchanged: e.g. 14. wants/is asking us to let
her know if we are   16. wants/is asking us to hang . . . when we are

Drill 99   (a) *He told us to* hang **our** coats up.   2. He told/warned us
not to write in the margin. Note nos. 15 and 18: 15. He told us to look
over our work before we handed it in.   18. He told us to go out quietly
when we'd finished.

(b) *He says we're to* hang **our** coats up. Or: *He wants us to* hang **our**
coats up.   2. He says we're not to write in the margin.   Or: He warns
us not to write in the margin.   Note that in nos. 15 and 18 the present
perfect tenses remain unchanged.

Drill 100   (a) *He says that* if one of the children loses his appetite *I am
to* take his temperature.

(b) *He said that* if one of the children lost his appetite *I was to* take his
temperature.   2. if his temperature was very high, I was to ring
3. if one of them cut himself, I was to wash . . .   4. when they had
finished . . . I was to let   5. when they were in bed, I was to read
6. if it got cold, I was to make   7. if they missed the school bus, I was
to send   8. when I went out, I was to double-lock   9. if the cat was
still out when I went to bed, I was to leave   10. if I hadn't time to
cook, I was to open   11. when I had used up . . . I was to buy
12. if I ran out of oil, I was to order   13. if it got colder, I was to turn
14. if the central heating didn't work properly, I was to phone
15. if the dogs wouldn't eat tinned food, I was to buy   16. if the dogs
barked . . . I was to go down and see what it was   17. if the tank
leaked, I was to send   18. if any letters came for him, I was to
forward   19. if the gardener turned up, I was to ask him   20. when
the milkman brought his bill, I was to pay it

116